HYDROPONICS FOR BEGINNERS

I0554778

The Ultimate Guide To Easily Start To Grow Vegetables,
Fruits And Herbs At Home And To Learn All About
Hydroponic Gardening And Aquaponics

Carole Smith

Legal & Disclaimer

The information contained in this book and its contents is not designed to replace or take the place of any form of medical or professional advice; and is not meant to replace the need for independent medical, financial, legal or other professional advice or services, as may be required. The content and information in this book have been provided for educational and entertainment purposes only.

The content and information contained in this book has been compiled from sources deemed reliable, and it is accurate to the best of the Author's knowledge, information and belief. However, the Author cannot guarantee its accuracy and validity and cannot be held liable for any errors and/or omissions. Further, changes are periodically made to this book as and when needed. Where appropriate and/or necessary, you must consult a professional (including but not limited to your doctor, attorney, financial advisor or such other professional advisor) before using any of the suggested remedies, techniques, or information in this book.

Upon using the contents and information contained in this book, you agree to hold harmless the Author from and against any damages, costs, and expenses, including any legal fees potentially resulting from the application of any of the information provided by this book. This disclaimer applies to any loss, damages or injury caused by the use and application, whether directly or indirectly, of any advice or information presented, whether for breach of contract, tort, negligence, personal injury, criminal intent, or under any other cause of action.

You agree to accept all risks of using the information presented inside this book.

You agree that by continuing to read this book, where appropriate and/or necessary, you shall consult a professional (including but not limited to your doctor, attorney, or financial advisor or such other advisor as needed) before using any of the suggested remedies, techniques, or information in this book.

TABLE OF CONTENTS

CHAPTER 1

WHAT IS HYDROPONIC CULTIVATION?

Hydroponic cultivation is a soilless cultivation technique for plants. It is an increasingly widespread system in agriculture that is also well suited to gardening and home horticulture.

By not altering the natural growth process of plants, hydroponics replaces the earth with an inert substrate from which plants get nourishment through their roots.

In aeroponic cultivation, on the other hand, the roots grow in contact with the air, in the absence of substrate, and are nourished through nebulization systems with water and nutrient solutions.

The hydroponic system is very versatile and allows anyone to create a garden or a small indoor vegetable garden, even in small spaces, without having to upset the home environment.

This technique allows even those who live in cities with little space, to create their own personal vegetable garden.

The cultivation systems without soil, in fact, are very simple and work thanks to the combination of some factors that give life to the small ecosystem in the greenhouse:

lighting with led light;

temperature and humidity;

substrate.

On the market there are several kits for the construction of mini-greenhouses, already complete with lighting with LED lamps and an irrigation system.

But first, you should first plan the type of crop you intend to grow and identify a space in which to place the kit.

Although it may seem complex, the method of growing indoors for flowering and garden plants is actually very simple. It is, in fact, a system that, once started, gives visible and rewarding results in a short time.

Once the hydroponic greenhouse is installed, you can move on to the next step to start cultivation with the chosen seedlings, the growing medium and the specific nutrient solution and fertilizers for each vegetative phase.

The substrate can generally be composed of expanded clay or coconut fiber.

The functions of the substrate are:

support the roots;

provide nourishment through the nutrient solution introduced into the irrigation system;

maintain constant humidity, while ensuring the passage of air and oxygenation of the roots themselves.

With hydroponic techniques, then, new seedlings are easily obtained from cuttings, as a favorable environment for rooting is created.

Hydroponics, among its many advantages, is not subject to seasonality. In fact, there is no need to limit yourself to vegetables available only in certain periods, but it is possible to grow fruit and vegetables all year round, maintaining a constant and adequate production to your needs.

In a corner of the kitchen, in the pantry or on the windowsill, the indoor vegetable garden guarantees a small, constant harvest that can be exploited for the creation of genuine and tasty dishes. With hydroponic cultivation, in fact, the products of the garden grow in a natural and healthy way, maintaining the characteristics of the flavor and organoleptic qualities unaltered.

It is enough to make a mini-soil of the right size for your needs and use the right products to improve the growth and production of plants.

And for the vegetable garden, the substrate is an important and decisive element for the correct development and good yield of plants. Vegetable plants, in fact, find "fertile soil" in the substrate composed of expanded clay (which guarantees oxygenation and correct drainage for the roots) and coconut fiber (which supports the plants and maintains the right humidity).

The plants, then, must be fed with the nutrient solution. In the substrate, in fact, the roots encounter less resistance and expand faster, also thanks to the immediately available and constantly present nourishment.

Managing a hydroponic garden is an exhilarating and also educational experience as it allows you to witness firsthand the birth and growth of seedlings and their fruits. In addition, an indoor vegetable garden allows you to grow a quantity of vegetables adequate to the space available and your personal need. It is an innovative technique that allows plants to develop safe from the attack of parasites and molds that frequently affect plant species grown indoors and outdoors in pots.

It is necessary to choose the fertilizers suitable for the vegetative cycle of the plants, pay attention to the dosage of the nutrient solution and keep under control the possible alterations of the pH and of the electrical conductivity, EC.

Thanks to the technique of hydroponics, gardening and horticulture at home becomes possible and easy to manage, even by those who live in the city and have little time to devote themselves to the care of greenery.

If you love a green lifestyle and don't want to give up the well-being that a small green oasis can bring into your home, you have to start a hydroponics culture.

To start an indoor cultivation project with hydroponics it takes very little:

A kit for hydroponics complete with lighting and irrigation system;

substrate;

instruments for checking the pH and EC values.

The actual cost varies according to the size of the kit and the options you decide to purchase. In any case, once the shopping is done, all the elements of the kit are reusable and recyclable, including the substrate which, once a crop cycle is finished, can be reconditioned for a new seeding (two or three times).

As already mentioned, with soilless cultivation, both flowering plants and vegetables are available and vigorous all year round and the substrate on which they are grown offers several advantages:

retains moisture and saves on water consumption for irrigation;

guarantees the absence of pathogenic fungi, molds and parasites;

supports the plants and allows the roots to grow quickly;

keeps vegetables healthy;

improves the quality of flowering of ornamental plants, the quantity of vegetables and aromatic herbs.

In short, hydroponic cultivation represents an optimal solution for growing a large variety of plants with minimum bulk and effort, maximum results and great satisfaction.

CHAPTER 2

BUILDING A HYDROPONIC GARDEN

Hydroponics is a word composed of "hydro" which means water and "ponia" which translates as work; that is, it is a soilless cultivation system. Although it has been modernized in recent times, it is known that about 2600 years ago, in Babylon, King Nebuchadnezzar I had the hanging gardens built in which plants were grown in this way.

Any plant worthy of its name needs light, water and a balanced amount of nutrients. These nutrients are absorbed regularly by the roots, whenever they are mixed with water or whenever they need them, thus achieving excellent health and optimal growth.

Although one might think that they can barely grow in this system, the truth is that it will depend a lot on the type of conglomerate and on how large the spaces intended for the plants are.

Types of hydroponic systems

It can be open or closed.

Open hydroponic system

The nutrient solution is mixed with water as often as needed, without being recycled, such as is done in grow beds or PVC pipes.

Closed hydroponic system

The nutrients circulate continuously, so that the roots can absorb them whenever they need it. This is what is done if it is grown in PVC channels, or with the Nutrient Film technique, among others.

What are the essential nutrients for plants?

Hydroponics is a growing system.

If we want our hydroponic system to function properly, it is essential to know what nutrients the plants need, otherwise they will not grow properly:

Macronutrients

Nitrogen (N): they use it to produce leaves and grow.

Posphorus (P): stimulates and promotes the growth of roots, flowers, fruits and seeds. It also helps fight disease.

Potassium (K): helps in the development of the stems and also to grow.

Sulfur (S): used for the formation of proteins and chlorophyll.

Calcium (Ca): responsible for the ability to transpire and helps protect against disease and stress due to high temperatures.

Magnesium (Mg): essential for the production of chlorophyll and, therefore, for photosynthesis.

Micronutrients

Chlorine (Cl): necessary for the photosynthetic reactions that oxygen produces.

Iron (Fe): essential for synthesizing chlorophyll.

Boron (B): intervenes in pollination and in the use of calcium.

Manganese (Mn): activates some enzymes and is needed to release oxygen in photosynthesis.

Zinc (Zn): part of the compound of some enzymes.

Copper (Cu): essential for respiration and necessary for the photosynthesis process. It also helps to intensify the flavor and color of vegetables and flowers.

Nickel (Ni): deals with metabolizing urea nitrogen to convert it into ammonia that can be used for plants.

Molybdenum (Mo): fixes nitrogen and reduces nitrates.

Knowing this, you can make a proper mix of nutrients, depending on the season you are in.

What are the requirements for having a hydroponic culture?

You need to take into account the following:

Position

The ideal site should be sunny, with at least six hours of sunlight. In addition, it must be away from sources of wind, diseased plants and pets.

As a matter of convenience, there needs to be a water source nearby and a safe area to store nutrients.

Temperature and humidity

The temperature must be between 20 and 24°C, so that the roots can easily absorb nutrients and the plants grow as well as possible. Humidity should be between 40 and 60%.

Water

Water is essential for life and when we want to have our own hydroponic cultivation it is even more important. It must be as pure and clean as possible. Hence, distilled water is preferred, with low electrical conductivity (EC) and low parts per million (PPM) levels.

Also, the pH should be between 5.8 and 6.2. pH measures the alkalinity of a solution on a scale from 0 to 14, considered acidic below 7, neutral at 7, and alkaline above 7.

Hydroponic fertilizers

Today, you will find ready-to-apply hydroponic nutrient solutions for sale, liquid or powdered. What you will see are three numbers, which indicate the proportion of NPK it contains. So, if it is 15-15-15, it indicates that it contains 15% nitrogen, another 15% phosphorus and another 15% potassium. The remaining 55% consists essentially of water and micronutrients.

Liquid fertilizers simply need to be mixed. Follow the instructions on the labels for this.

Lighting

Plants need light to carry out photosynthesis and, therefore, also to grow, flower, bear fruit ... and ultimately, to be alive. Knowing this, they should be given 15 to 18 hours of light a day in full growth and between 10 to 12 hours a day during flowering.

How to get it? With MH lamps. These lamps emit a blue-green spectrum of light which is ideal for the growth phase. If you plan on growing cuttings as well, or short-lived plants, they will do best with T5 lighting, which is a high-performance fluorescent light that has very low power consumption.

Make sure it always turns on and off at the same time every day. There are special timers. This is to avoid imbalances in the development or growth of plants.

Dimensions

Available space is not something you should worry about. There are very small hydroponic gardens, 1m, and there are larger ones up to 200m. So if you don't have a very big place, don't worry because even in a small space you can have a productive crop.

Containers

In fact, anything non-metallic that is waterproof and at least 10cm deep can do the trick: tires, plastic buckets, wooden boxes. Better to use dark, dull-colored containers, as algae tend to develop best in those that are light colors.

Substrates for hydroponics

The substrates to be used must be new, pristine and capable of retaining moisture and draining excess water. Likewise, they must be composed of small particles, of between 2 and 7 mm, and must not degrade easily. Therefore, the following mixtures are recommended:

50% akadama + 50% previously washed river sand

60% pumice + 40% arlite

Hydroponics is a growing system in which diseases are easily preventable.

Benefits

Traditional plant cultivation is a very interesting and educational option, but the truth is that compared to hydroponics, it has minor advantages:

Pests and diseases are prevented

By using clean substrates and water, pests and disease-causing microorganisms are prevented from appearing and, even if they do, they are easier to eliminate. Thus, much healthier and stronger harvests are obtained.

The same species can be grown over and over again

The highest yields are obtained in the same space.

There are several systems in which many specimens can be planted. And since each of them will have the amount of nutrients they need, we can be sure they will all ripen.

You get healthier plants

Since we have the task of providing them with everything they need, they are able to have a balanced supply of light, air, water and, of course, nutrients.

There is no need to use earth

Water, as long as it is clean, is an excellent medium in which plants can grow. What's more, you can fully control the available nutrients and they can be reused while staying in the system.

Disadvantages

A constant water supply is required

Without water, no plant will grow. Remember that hydroponics means growing without soil, but if this precious liquid is not available, nothing will be achieved.

It takes time

You have to study to learn everything, to take care of plants and for the prevention and treatment of pests and diseases.

The initial investment can be high

A complete, professional kit costs you at least €400. But it is money that you end up recovering over time, since you will not have the need to spend it on plant protection products if you take the utmost care of the details, and check that both the water, the support and the system are clean. In addition, you also save the cost of buying the food that, from seeds, you will get ... and those bags of seeds currently cost 1-2 euros.

By now you probably think hydroponics is reserved for professionals only, but the reality is that that's not entirely true. It requires some technical knowledge, but that doesn't mean this is a world that amateurs can't enter.

You can have your own hydroponic garden in a simple 2-liter bottle. You do not believe me? Follow these steps and then tell me:

Materials

2l bottle

Coconut fiber

1 liter of water

1-2 wicks of fabric

Aluminum sheet

1l of fertilizer for hydroponics

Small vegetable seeds: tomatoes, peppers, lettuce, basil, ...

Permanent marker

Scissors

pH corrector kit

Step by step

First, clean the bottle thoroughly, with water.

Then, mark a line with the marker, about 5 cm below the hole, where the curvature of the bottle disappears.

Now, cut the bottle along the line and place the cut part inside, upside down. Fill the lower half with water until you see that it almost covers the narrowest part of the part you introduced.

The next step is to add the wick, passing it through the mouth of the bottle and making it reach about two thirds of the height of the area that will be used for growth, i.e. the top.

The wick should be more or less in the center.

Finally, sow two or three seeds, leaving them somewhat separated from each other. Later, when they have grown a little - 2 or 3 weeks after sowing - choose the strongest.

So that the garden is free of pests and diseases, wrap the bottle with something opaque, such as aluminum foil.

CHAPTER 3

BRIEF HISTORY FROM THE BABYLONIANS TO THE SECOND WORLD WAR

For those who have already heard of hydroponics it will be difficult to imagine this innovative-looking method being used by the Babylonians and Aztecs, yet this could be its origin.

What if we told you that there is a method to grow your favorite plants in less time, consuming less energy, less water, but increasing productivity per meter while guaranteeing healthy and safe products? Yes, it is said that even in one of the seven wonders, the gardens of Babylon, this system was applied successfully. In fact, hydroponics is a cultivation technique with innovative appearances but which has its roots in history.

The history of hydroponics, from the Babylonians to the Aztecs

Before we get to the heart of the matter and discover the benefits of hydroponic cultivation, let's take a look at its surprising history. The first hints of a similar system are found in the structure of the Hanging Gardens of Babylon. In fact, some scholars believe that the secret behind the success of such an amazing structure was the application of this technique, obviously without awareness of the underlying mechanisms.

Another important piece to reconstruct the history of hydroponics is the testimonies reported by Marco Polo, who describes the 'floating gardens' used by the Chinese to grow plants on the surface of the water, a technique extremely similar to that which will be discovered to be used by the Aztecs. a couple of centuries later, on Lake Tenochititlan with their 'chinampas'.

During these four centuries the commitment of the still immature 'scientific community' was to develop a series of cultivation techniques suitable not so much to maximize agronomic results, but more to investigate the functioning of plants, their way of eating.

In 1600 the approach actually becomes more scientific and experimental, we try to understand how plant nutrition can actually work. The Belgian, Jan Van Helmont, scientifically demonstrated how water was essential for the survival of the plant and that from this the plant drew most of the substances it needed.

In the following three centuries, many theories were advanced on the scientific assumptions behind the relatively complex metabolism of plants, it was discovered that they need water, light and air to survive, in particular thanks to macro and micro nutrients present in the soil. In the early 1900s, studies further intensified, until, during the Second World War, American soldiers stationed in the Pacific islands used hydroponics where it was not possible to plow, so much so that in the locality of Chofu, 22 hectares of land were cultivated in this way.

A new start thanks to plastic

Interest, however, remained largely dormant until 1970, when we began to work with plastic materials: up to that moment, in fact, the beds in which the hydroponic plants were grown had to be built in cement, making the plants very expensive. With the introduction of plastic, however, this trend was interrupted, rekindling the spotlight on a technique that had yet to demonstrate its full potential.

And so we come to the present day, where hydroponic cultivation is used all over the world, although not at the pace that might have been expected. In fact, until now it has been more efficient, for most crops and nations, to remain faithful to traditional systems, even if this trend is not destined to last: the increasingly limited spaces, the resources to be used sparingly are all factors that push in the direction of a new, old, more efficient system.

CHAPTER 4

CHLOROPHYLL PHOTOSYNTHESIS

What do plants and humans have in common?

Mmmm. Difficult to say ... maybe they are all living beings? Yes, true.

Are they both green? Unless one of you is the Hulk, I would say no (in case there is: feel free to change this answer, as long as you don't get angry! ... For heaven's sake)

Do they breathe? Yes, but in a different way.

So what? Well, if we told you right away we would ruin the suspense, so read through, we're going to shed some light on some memories buried in your memory!

But first it is essential to shed some light on some characteristics that will help us better understand the world of plants.

So let's start talking about this fascinating topic!

Plants are organisms called "autotrophs". What does that mean? Simply that they are able to independently produce the material necessary for survival.

Unlike "heterotrophic" beings, that is, primary consumers (herbivorous animals) and secondary (omnivorous) consumers, plants do not need to eat other beings to sustain themselves. They create their food through photosynthesis.

THE CHLOROPHILLIAN PHOTOSYNTHESIS

Photosynthesis is a complex and fundamental procedure for life but, before talking about it, it is useful to do a little in-depth analysis: it may seem that the universe is "man-centered". That it is based on what it takes to allow humans and animals to live in comfortable conditions. However, this is not the case. The conditions that animal life found when the earth was inhabited by plants and some microorganisms dictated the law.

It is no coincidence that oxygen is in the air and that we need just that to breathe. We have molded ourselves, like all other life forms, following what we have found. Consequently it was the plants that made us develop in this specific way, preparing an atmosphere full of their waste product: oxygen.

Well, now let's get straight to the point and focus on photosynthesis!

WHAT IS CHLOROPHILLIAN PHOTOSYNTHESIS?

Chlorophyll photosynthesis is a biochemical process, which aims to create and store energy for the plant. It will use the energy gained to grow, create new leaves, and so on.

This process resides in the leaves (generally in all green parts of the plant). We can think of leaves as natural solar panels. Inside the green tissues, the plant hosts small organisms called chloroplasts, inside which a substance known as chlorophyll flows.

CHLOROPHYL

The substance that gives plants their typical green color. It is found mainly in the leaves, but when a plant is very young it is often also present in the stem. It is able to intercept the sun's rays and harness the energy that comes from them.

SUNLIGHT

Here is another basic ingredient. Once the light is intercepted by the chlorophyll it is able to supply the energy necessary to combine carbon dioxide and water to form sugars (carbohydrates), that is the fundamental nourishment of the plant.

CARBON DIOXIDE

Carbon dioxide, or CO_2, is an absolutely odorless gas that is produced by animals (including humans) during respiration but can derive from other phenomena such as combustion.

It is quite harmful and is the main greenhouse gas in the earth's atmosphere. Do not worry, it is not too dangerous, but in very large quantities it can do the greatest damage.

Despite these negative notes it also has good aspects: it is able to intercept the infrared radiation (heat) of sunlight, then reflecting it towards our planet, thus preventing the Earth from undergoing a large temperature difference between day and night. A kind of blanket for the planet. However, the excessive production of CO_2 from human activities has turned this blanket into a shroud, causing global warming.

WATER

We all know water: with its famous formula H_2O, it is a fundamental constituent of life on our planet.

In fact, water is a basic reagent for this process to take place.

OXYGEN

Oxygen is what we animals breathe, it's fundamental for the life of our entire ecosystem.

The plant absorbs carbon dioxide and water to create energy in the form of sugars. The leaves expel the waste of this reaction, which is oxygen. Without plants, the production of oxygen would cease, making the Earth unlivable.

SAP

The vector for plant nutrition (a bit like our blood). It travels inside the plants, crossing the phloem and xylem.

There are two types:

Raw sap: consists largely of mineral salts and water. It starts from the roots and rises (against the force of gravity) up to the leaves, passing through the conducting vessels of the plants.

Elaborated sap: mainly composed of water, sucrose (sugar) and mineral salts. While the raw sap is transported linearly from the bottom to the top, the processed sap can flow in both directions.

The process of photosynthesis is first of all divided into 2 phases:

Luminous phase: the solar energy we were talking about changes into chemical energy. It means that it is divided into two types of chemical compounds:

ATP: carries energy and allows the generation of some metabolic functions and the creation of carbohydrates;

NADPH2: transfers electrons, usually the hydrogen ion H+, to then create the synthesis of carbohydrates with other components.

Dark phase: carbon dioxide turns into glucose.

From the name, one could guess that they are phases extremely linked to the presence / absence of light, but, in reality, only one is. The luminous phase requires the presence of the sun, as sunlight must be absorbed by the chlorophyll and then transformed into useful energy. The dark phase, on the other hand, can occur at any time. That is, when there is no direct sunlight.

It will seem strange but perhaps everything will be clearer by looking at the chemical formula:

CO_2 (carbon dioxide) + H_2O (water) = (CH_2O (carbohydrates)) + O_2

Ok, perhaps it is not yet very clear, here is a practical example:

$6 CO_2 + 6 H_2O = C_6H_{12}O_6 + 6 O_2$

6 molecules of carbon dioxide + 6 molecules of water equals 1 molecule of glucose + 6 molecules of oxygen.

So 6 molecules of carbon dioxide plus 6 molecules of water

produce 1 molecule of glucose plus six of oxygen.

WHAT IS IT FOR?

Its ultimate purpose is to create nourishment for the plant. But, in more detail, the aim is to create glucose, which is necessary to release the fundamental energies for the metabolic processes essential for plants.

The excess carbon dioxide is absorbed by the plants, limiting the polluting elements present in the air.

With the ever-growing world of industry and heavy logging practices, the way forward is destroying the basic foundations of our life. Carbon dioxide is constantly increasing, produced by factories and industry and, at the same time, we are significantly reducing the vegetation which, after all, is the only great defense we have, precisely because it is able to transform the harmful anhydride into useful oxygen.

It is strange to think about, but by dint of undermining the environment we are preparing a world full of things, but inhospitable for human life itself.

Photosynthesis is a biochemical process, so it is not easy to explain and understand, but let's try to summarize the main steps.

The water and mineral salts found in the soil are absorbed by the roots.

The substances take the form of raw sap and rise along the stem (or stem) of the plant, reaching the leaves.

Once at their destination, the leaves begin to absorb the carbon dioxide present in the air through the stomata.

When sunlight lands on the leaves, true chlorophyll photosynthesis takes place: the raw sap and carbon dioxide are transformed into processed sap.

Once photosynthesis has been completed, the plant, again through the stomata, releases oxygen into the atmosphere.

Then the glucose and mineral salts are brought, still in the form of elaborated sap, to all parts of the plant. Especially the roots.

IS IT BETTER NOT TO KEEP THE PLANTS IN THE BEDROOM?

This is something that we often hear, everyone knows that for some reason it is not a healthy practice to put plants in the environment where you sleep.

But is it true? The answer is yes. The motivation is found in the dark phase of photosynthesis.

Once sunlight is no longer present, the plants stop absorbing carbon dioxide and, consequently, releasing oxygen, reversing the process. Oxygen is withdrawn, leaving carbon dioxide in exchange.

This alone is enough to make you understand how unhealthy it is. During the night the plants decrease oxygen levels, while we are sleeping.

OTHER MOLECULES?

All the more complex substances that will then make up the tissues of the plant, such as phosphorus, are absorbed by the soil through the roots.

In conclusion, let's try to answer the question we asked ourselves earlier: what do plants and humans have in common?

Rather, they need mutual respect, because, otherwise, neither species could survive.

Sounds like a bit of a cliché phrase, huh? Well, maybe it really is, but that doesn't rule out the truth behind it. Plants provide us with the fundamental ingredient for our survival, the least we can do is not to alter their environment, allowing them to grow in the best way.

CHAPTER 5

BEFORE WE BEGIN

Essential tools for growing with hydroponics

1. What I need to start hydroponic cultivation

In this first part of the guide, dedicated to what is needed to start a hydroponic cultivation, we will consider all the necessary tools in the three phases, of germination, growth and for the final flowering phase and the indicative costs to be faced in order to start a hydroponic cultivation at home or in the greenhouse.

But what are the costs to be incurred to start hydroponic agriculture?

Establishing the final and exact cost of hydroponic cultivation is not that simple, because there are a series of variables that affect the final price. However, it is possible to have a rough idea to be able to orientate yourself. For a private individual who wants to start hydroponic cultivation at home, the cost to be incurred - for a basic starter kit - ranges between 400 and 500 euros, while if you want a more complex system, using the latest discoveries and highly technological products in terms of lamps, boxes and extractors, it can reach €1,000 / 1,100.

For those who wish, instead, to start real hydroponic agriculture at a professional level, the costs vary considerably, due to a greater number of factors to be considered in setting up the system. They range from a minimum of 200 euros up to a maximum of 1000 euros, but of course it must be considered that these are indicative price ranges and that - in any case - the more the cultivated greenhouse area increases, the lower the average cost.

So, let's take a closer look at what it takes to build a plant and start hydroponic cultivation.

For the Germination Phase:

Necessary

Mini greenhouse (in which to germinate the seeds)

Rockwool cubes (at least 1 for each seed you want to germinate)

Root stimulator

Optional

Neon light

Watertight heating element (to keep the temperature of the mini-earth stable at the optimum temperature of about 26 degrees)

For the Growth and Flowering Phase:

Necessary

Indoor Lighting Kit (in a separate chapter we will explain how to choose the lighting system)

Light bulb

Power supply

Lamp / Reflector Holder

Hydroponic System

Expanded clay

pH test

EC test

pH corrector

Nutriments for the growth phase

Nourishment for the flowering phase

Timer

Optional

Thermometer / hygrometer

Grow Box / Grow Room or Mylar sheet

Humidifier

Fan

The equipment you will need is important. In the absence of soil, you will have to ensure your plants have everything they need to grow and flower in a reasonable time.

During the germination phase, you need a sufficiently porous, solid, inert substrate. You can choose between:

Expanded clay, a material that is used in both agriculture and construction, a mineral of volcanic origin that owes its name to the characteristic worm shape it takes when heated;

Rock wool (a very versatile drainage material);

Coconut fiber (a light, ecological and recyclable substrate).

A mini-greenhouse that guarantees a high level of humidity (used to germinate the seeds);

A root stimulator (based on amino acids and vitamins);

A watertight heating resistance system (to keep the temperature of the mini-greenhouse always stable, around 26 degrees).

According to the information found on specialized sites, there are solutions for every type of pocket:

A Start kit costs less than 10 euros;

A Basic kit costs just over 28 euros;

An Advanced kit costs almost 90 euros;

A Professional kit costs almost 240 euros.

During the growth and flowering phase, you need:

An indoor lighting kit (which includes the lamp, reflector and magnetic ballast). It has a cost ranging from 68.73 euros (for 150 Watts) to 187.16 euros (for 1,000 Watts);

A hydroponic system (includes all the components useful for making plants flourish and grow, including the immersion pump through which the nutrient solution is transmitted). It has a cost ranging from 58.90 euros to over one thousand euros;

A pH meter (used to measure the acidity and alkalinity levels present in the water. The optimal value should be between 5.8 and 6.0). A Basic pH kit costs on average 12.90 euros, an Advanced pH kit, 56 euros and a Professional pH kit almost 150 euros;

An EC meter (used to measure the electrical conductivity of the solutions or the quantity of mineral salts dissolved in the water). An Eco kit costs 39 euros, a Pro kit exceeds 117 euros while an EC Regulator / Doser (which does not limit itself to measuring the value, but intervenes automatically if needed) can cost more than 900 euros;

Nutrients for the growth and flowering phase (they are fertilizers that help plant growth). They cost between 10 and 40 euros;

Some humidifiers or fans (useful for maintaining optimal air conditions).

Hydroponic cultivation is a cultivation that is often practiced in an enclosed environment called the Grow Room. Do not just equip it properly, but also take care to constantly monitor the internal conditions, paying attention to:

Light: during the growth phase, the plant needs about 18 hours of light a day;

Temperature: the optimal "climate" in a grow room is between 21 and 28 degrees;

Humidity: it must be around 50-60%. Be careful not to go above as an excessively humid environment favors the onset of molds that can damage plants and compromise your crop.

CHAPTER 6

PRACTICAL HYDROPONIC PLANTS: TYPES, LIST OF EXAMPLES AND HOW TO GROW THEM.

To begin with, let's make it clear that when we talk about hydroponic plants, we are really referring not to one type of plant, but to a way of growing plants that can thrive very well with this technique. Hydroponic cultivation consists of producing plants without using the soil. The plant grows only in water, where it finds all the nutrients it needs for cultivation.

Hydroponic cultivation is applicable to almost all plant species, especially for ornamental species, since thanks to it, the flowers are kept longer. However, although it is practiced more every day, as we have seen it is very ancient: the Aztecs practiced it in their floating gardens.

List of examples of hydroponic plants

As we mentioned, virtually any plant can be grown hydroponically. This technique is increasingly used lazily by some gardening and horticulture lovers.

However, in some territories where the land is not fertile or there is not an abundance of land but of water, hydroponic cultivation can become an integral part of the industry, as in addition to producing more nutrient-rich and healthier foods, they ripen in less time.

lettuce

tomato

pepper

spinach

mint

celery

mint

sage

basil

marjoram

valerian

ginger

lavender

parsley

garlic

Hydroponics is the agriculture of the future because it produces healthier and more nutritious crops, optimizing the resources provided to the plant better, as well as requiring less fertilizer and pesticide. In this other article we explain more about hydroponics, a more ecological and sustainable agriculture.

To get started you will need a home hydroponic kit, which you can buy in specialty stores or install yourself.

In this guide, we will also show you how to make your own kit. One that you have probably seen in photographs or videos is the NFT hydroponic system, which is very striking to operate through a series of pipes and channels that are arranged in multiple rows like a vertical garden. In them, the nutrient solution is in constant circulation, so that the water never stagnates and the plant always gets what it needs.

As for the care of growing hydroponic plants at home, apart from the technique with water, each species or type of hydroponic plant can have different needs, so it is recommended to buy seeds or campuses ask the store specialist for the needs specifics of said plant (light, temperature, nutrients, etc.).

To finish talking about growing hydroponic plants, let's explain how to easily make a homemade hydroponic growing. To do this, you will need the following:

Homemade hydroponics materials

An air pump. It will not be easy to manufacture. It serves to oxygenate the water, such as those used in aquariums. Without this oxygenation of the water, the roots will not develop properly and could lead to contamination of the water. Therefore, it is best to acquire one.

An opaque container. A box, bowl, large tube, or other container with sufficient depth. It must be opaque because the roots require darkness.

Sprouted seeds. You can germinate them yourself or buy them prepared.

Drill a hole in the bottom of the chosen container. It must be covered with a plastic cap or waterproof material.

Fill the container with water, without reaching the top. In parallel, prepare the lid of the container by drilling a few holes, all of the same size.

Place the shoots in the holes, so that the roots are well covered with water, then fix them with the substrate. Some popular hydroponic substrates are pumice and gravel.

Place your hydroponics in a lighted area. Better, however, if in the most intense light hours, it does not reach the plants directly. Do not forget to add the oxygenator to the water and program it to activate it at least a few minutes every 3 hours. Also, add a hydroponics nutrient solution to the water and substrate. Here, each species has its own needs.

CHAPTER 7
HYDROPONICS VERSUS TRADITIONAL CULTURE

Hydroponics or earth? Here are the differences

S oilless cultivation is a relatively recent technique that has brought great benefits to the agricultural sector, especially in countries with extreme climatic conditions. Even at home, hydroponic cultivation has many advantages and is a valid alternative to gardening and horticulture on the ground.

With hydroponic cultivation, then, it is possible to create small indoor gardens and vegetable gardens, even in an apartment or in a city, taking advantage of the available space without bulky superstructures or accessories. The kits for hydroponic greenhouses recreate the ideal environmental and climatic conditions for the cultivation of a large variety of plants.

Hydroponics, or soilless cultivation

Soilless cultivation is a cultivation system in substrate or in liquid medium (hydroponics).

In agriculture, on an industrial scale and globally, hydroponics is a relatively recent technique which, however, has immediately found success, especially in areas of the world where climatic and physical adversities of the territory make most of the crops for food use difficult and unsustainable.

In many countries, hydroponic greenhouses for the extensive cultivation of vegetables represent the ideal solution to meet the needs of the population and safeguard agricultural production.

Soilless cultivation systems have proven to be particularly suitable for growing vegetables. Hydroponic crops have better growth and development than land-grown vegetables. Greenhouse cultivation, then, allows growers to have a generous and constant harvest to meet the demands of the market throughout the year. The use of LED lamps and other tools is essential to recreate the ideal microclimate for the cultivation of typically summer vegetables. Hydroponics, on a global level, represented an eco-sustainable turning point for horticultural production on a global scale.

The principles on which the functioning of hydroponic systems is based are always the same:

Cultivation of plants on the basis of an inert substrate;

Microclimate all year round obtained by lighting with LED lights;

Nourishment for plants through specific nutrient solutions.

Hydroponics, therefore, in addition to presenting important opportunities for agriculture, also offers many advantages for indoor gardening and horticulture.

Hydroponics or earth: which one to choose?

Gardening and the cultivation of the home vegetable garden are rewarding and satisfying practices.

Especially for those who have a garden or a terrace available, the cultivation of ornamental plants and vegetables allows you to create green and fragrant corners to enjoy during the spring and summer season.

Cultivation in the soil is simple and immediate, but requires a certain knowledge of plant cultivation techniques and their specific needs regarding exposure, sowing period, flowering and fruit harvest.

The cultivation of plants on the ground and outdoors is subject to seasonality and unpredictable climatic variations.

The soil, then, must still be fertilized and treated so that it can offer nourishment, without water stagnation and pH alterations.

Growing without soil, both indoors and outdoors, can use a substrate with draining characteristics, capable of supporting the roots and letting the air pass through. The substrate, fertigated with the suitable nutrient solution, provides the plants with the nutrients necessary for their growth, improving the quantity and quality of flower or fruit production.

The substrate that replaces the earth is generally composed of:

Expanded clay;

Sand;

Coconut fiber.

Hydroponics is more suitable than soil cultivation because it requires less maintenance and clearly limits infestations by insects or parasites.

The hydroponic technique, then, has many advantages for indoor cultivation: it is hygienic and not dirty with soil residues, it does not produce unpleasant odors and it is very versatile since the plant can be placed in any domestic environment.

Germination: what is the difference between ground and soilless cultivation?

It can be germinated in water. The special substrate, in fact, once irrigated with the nutrients and minerals best suited to the types of plant chosen, is able to support plants in all their growth and vegetative phases.

In soil cultivation the soil must always be fertilized and treated so that parasites, insects, molds or fungi do not attack the seeds or sprouts.

In hydroponic cultivation the seeds, or sprouts, must be planted in the special substrate that has the power to offer the seed, or the tender roots, the right support and nourishment to develop quickly.

The suitable substrate has a remarkable draining capacity and, at the same time, manages to retain the substances of the fertilizers to nourish the seedlings in a constant and homogeneous way.

In indoor cultivation it is also possible to recreate the ideal climate for the germination of plants, without seasonality constraints.

Even in agriculture, hydroponic cultivation has several advantages over ground cultivation. The same advantages are also present on a smaller scale, such as in gardening and in the care of the home vegetable garden.

As already mentioned, compared to crops with the earth, the culture with the substrate is more hygienic and guarantees greater cleanliness in the environment.

The hydroponic greenhouse, complete with LED light and irrigation, recreates the ideal environment to allow plants to grow in the best conditions: from germination, to vegetative development, to flowering or fruit production.

The following elements determine the success of your crop:

Lighting and temperature, calibrated on the type of cultivation;

pH of the substrate;

Balanced nutrition;

Constant humidity and no stagnation of water.

Once fully operational, the hydroponic greenhouse more than compensates the initial investment for its installation, as it minimizes the consumption of water and fertilizers. Furthermore, all the elements, once the life cycle of the plants has ended, are recyclable and reusable for a new crop.

Urban hydroponic cultivation is ideal for those with limited space available, as it easily adapts to every need. A home garden of aromatic and medicinal herbs, for example, constitutes a small resource for the needs of families: a small green oasis of perfumes and relaxation from which to draw whenever you want.

Hydroponic cultivation, therefore, is eco-sustainable and economical, suitable for those with a green thumb, but also for those who are not familiar with gardening; it is versatile and adaptable to any domestic environment, it gives satisfaction and well-being to the whole family.

CHAPTER 8
AQUAPONICS

What is aquaponics?

Have you ever heard of aquaculture or, more specifically, of agriculture by aquaponics? For many the term is obscure but the concept is quite simple. It is essentially a particular water cultivation technique that is carving out its own space in the world of agriculture.

But what is aquaponics in detail? What does it consist of, how does it work, what strengths and weaknesses does it have? And above all, is it a type of sustainable and organic cultivation or not?

Thanks to climate change and the international economic crisis, the need for the agri-food sector to identify new strategies to ensure more sustainable production in line with the new market needs appears evident.

What is aquaponics?

Aquaponics can be defined as the union between aquaculture and hydroponic cultivation. The latter is a practice in which plants are grown in the absence of soil, with only the use of water enriched with all the nutrients that the plants need. In the case of aquaponics, the essential nutrients for plant growth are provided by fish farming, of which these substances are the main waste products. In this system, elements such as nitrogen and phosphorus, deriving both from the excretion of the fish and from the decomposition of the feed not ingested, can be absorbed by the roots of the cultivated plants which are directly immersed in the water.

Aquaponics is not a new cultivation technique, in fact it was in the 70s that we began to talk substantially about this technique. However, it is only in recent years that it has returned to the fore, also thanks to new scientific research and the greater attention to sustainability on the part of consumers and producers.

Aquaponics cycle

How does aquaponics work?

An aquaponic system is a recirculation system, where the water, thanks to the use of one or more pumps, is taken from the tank in which the fish are raised and passed into a biofilter. This starts the nitrification process which will lead to the formation of nitrites and nitrates which are then assimilated by plants. The water is then introduced into the culture beds inside which the cultivated vegetables are present (whose roots are in direct contact with the water) and finally reintroduced into the breeding tank.

There are many plant varieties that can be grown, not only leafy vegetables but also plants such as zucchini, eggplant, tomatoes and aromatic herbs. Similarly, it is possible to breed almost all freshwater fish species in aquaponics, from trout to carp (but also ornamental species such as Koi carp) or even exotic species such as tilapia. It is also possible to breed various species of crustaceans in aquaponics. Make sure your plants get the right amount of nutrients.

Aquaponics can be understood as a sustainable agricultural production activity in which the cycles of the main macro-nutrients are closed thanks to the integration of two production systems, aquaculture and hydroponic cultivation. Compared to conventional farming techniques, aquaponics has several strengths, including:

Water saving: aquaponics uses about 90% less water than that used in traditional agriculture;

Small spaces: since the plants do not need soil, aquaponics allows intensive cultivation in relatively limited spaces;

No use of pesticides: aquaponics do not provide for their use;

No use of fertilizers: plant nutrients are provided by fish farming;

Emissions control: there is no need to use agricultural vehicles with consequent lower consumption of fossil fuels.

The main limitations of aquaponics concern two fundamental aspects: the complexity of the production system and its economic sustainability. Being an integrated production system, aquaponics requires skills on the part of the farmer / breeder both as regards the cultivation of plant species and in the context of fish farming.

From an economic point of view, aquaponics is able to generate a double profit for those who practice it, with the placing on the market of two different types of products (vegetables and fish). On the other hand, the need to allocate these systems inside greenhouses or protected structures and to condition the temperature in order to guarantee constant production throughout the year, increase production costs. But at the moment this is the price that the consumer has to get used to paying for a truly sustainable product.

Domestic aeroponics

The ideal solution for people with small spaces who want to approach aeroponic cultivation are ready-made kits, also for sale on the web.

Accompanied by simple instructions, they are divided according to the level with which you want to compare for this type of crop. The 400w Indoor Aeroponic Kit is a favorite of all growers and can also be purchased on Amazon.

Aeroponic cultivation, for indoor cultivation

As in extended crops, also in this case the nutrients are absorbed by the roots by nebulization, through small capillary ducts, which can be activated with an automatic timer.

The nutrients must be carefully dosed to ensure the right amount of microelements that will allow the plants to grow luxuriant and strong.

The plant is inserted in disks that maintain the aerial roots, suitable for indoor cultivation and designed to be used in cultivation kits such as indoor cultivation Grow Boxes and starter kits for aeroponic cultivation.

CHAPTER 9
HOW TO BUILD A GREENHOUSE AT HOME

Today, having a small greenhouse in your home is possible: just make a DIY Grow Box. Let's find out together what is needed and how to build a Grow Box to plant what we want in our home.

There are different ways to make a DIY vegetable garden, and they can adapt to all needs. Those who have a beautiful garden can build a splendid synergistic vegetable garden, while those who have a balcony or a terrace could think of a DIY vertical vegetable garden. A very popular technique, simple and applicable even at home is also hydroponic cultivation. To carry out hydroponic cultivation at home, however, we will need a small domestic greenhouse, or a Grow Box.

A Grow Box is a small structure, equipped with some important tools, which will allow us to grow any plant even indoors. There are several ready-made kits available to build a Grow Box. However, for those who want to save money and put their manual skills to good use, it is possible to build a perfect DIY Grow Box. So let's find out what you need and how to proceed to build a DIY Grow

Box.

DIY Grow Box: what you need

We will need several essential elements that will then be assembled. First of all, we will need a structure in which to insert the plants and the instrumentation. The structure can be of different types depending on our needs and the dimensions we want to obtain. We can use a wardrobe, a cardboard box, an emptied computer case or we can build our structure using metal or PVC tubing and a plastic sheet.

To choose the size of the structure we must keep in mind that between the tips of the plants and the lamps (which we will place on the "ceiling" of the greenhouse) there must be a space of at least 40 cm (for LED lamps, even 20 cm is enough).

Mylar Sheets (or kitchen aluminum to save)

Lamp, socket and reflector

Programmable timer

Ventilation fan

Aspirator with flexible hose

Electric wires and adhesive tape

At this point we can assemble our DIY Grow Box. First, we have to insert the lamp in the center of the "ceiling" of the Grow Box, in order to guarantee uniform lighting. The number of lamps and their power depends on how many plants we want to plant and their species, as well as the size of the Grow Box itself. The lamp will be connected to the timer, in order to automatically manage the hours of light to be provided to the plants. The recommended minimum is 12 hours of light per day, but it can be up to a maximum of 20 hours for short periods.

At this point we can install the aspirator with the flexible hose in the lower part of the Grow Box (on one side). To let the saturated air out of the greenhouse. We can therefore also insert the fan (more or less at half height), which will allow the movement of air inside the Grow Box. These two tools will also allow us to better regulate the temperature, humidity and air exchange inside the greenhouse. These parameters will in fact be kept at the optimal values for the type of plant we have chosen to grow. To keep them under control we can therefore insert a thermometer and a humidity sensor.

Finally, if the internal surface of your Box is not already reflective, we will have to cover it with silver Mylar sheets or aluminum film. Spread the sheets well, in order to guarantee constant and homogeneous lighting for our plants. At this point we are ready to set up our DIY Grow Box, placing our plants inside with an attached hydroponic system (very convenient since it does not need to be watered by hand) or even simply in pots. The classic plants suitable for the Grow Box are for example chilli, basil or parsley in pots.

However, remember that there are many complete kits available to start growing immediately.

CHAPTER 10

HUMIDITY AND TEMPERATURE IN THE

GROW BOX

What is the fundamental point from which to start when we approach indoor cultivation in a Grow Box? It is important to try to recreate an environment that is healthy for the plants. This means that temperature and humidity will become the two basic parameters from which to start.

You must know that even the most advanced techniques for growing indoors can be irrelevant if these two values are not checked. At the environmental level, in fact, it will always be necessary to take into account any sudden changes, unexpected climatic conditions and act accordingly. Moreover, without a careful program that allows them to be organized, you will not be able to count on the success of cultivation. And this affects the quality and good flowering of the plants.

Relative humidity in the Grow Box

The first clarification to make is on the measurement of these two factors: the temperature is in degrees and the humidity is a percentage. If we let the latter reach 100%, our Grow Box will not be able to absorb water vapor. It will in fact be saturated and the water will settle between the walls, leaves and vases. Unfortunately, humidity is the most delicate factor, as it is difficult to understand how much there is in the air. It is no coincidence that we will speak of "relative humidity" because it is not an absolute value. The ability of air to retain water vapor is relative and alters according to the temperature. Generally hot air holds more moisture, while cold air holds less. The important thing is to find the right balance!

For example, if the humidity goes over 90%, the air fills with water and we will not have the correct transpiration from the stomata of the leaves. In this way, you risk running into mold and mildew. If, on the other hand, the humidity drops below 40%, the plant closes the stomata. Also, in this case we will not have the correct perspiration and the growth rate slows down.

Ideal temperature and humidity in the Grow Box

The humidity to be maintained to maximize indoor cultivation must be faithful to these values:

During the germination phase: humidity at 80%;

In the vegetative phase: between 60% and 70%;

At the time of flowering: between 50% and 60%.

As for the temperature, you will have to refer to these parameters:

During the germination phase: between 18° and 24°C;

In the growth phase: between 14° and 29°C;

At the time of the flowering phase: between 14° and 27°C.

The importance of the thermo-hygrometer

The thermo-hygrometer will therefore be very important in order to always give a value to the humidity in the grow room. In fact, with time and with the right experience, you learn about the typical characteristics of the Grow Box, adapting the environment to the needs of the plants. For example, if we have the same amount of water vapor in two different environments, do you know what could happen? In a hot environment the air will hold more water vapor and the thermo-hygrometer will give a humidity value that is lower than in an environment kept at a cold temperature.

A delicate point is the transition from day to night, at which time the values could suddenly become unbalanced. When we turn off the lamp, or the timer guarantees us this step, the bulb will stop heating. In this way the air and the temperature in the Grow Box will go down. It is a matter of a few minutes. If this step occurs too quickly, the humidity level can rise and touch dangerous values.

But now let's move on to the practice, after having illustrated the fundamental notions of this topic. To lower the humidity there are special ventilation systems. All you have to do is increase the flow of fresh air by choosing the size of the inlet itself. Also, try watering when the lights come on. And finally, it might be worthwhile to make a small investment by buying a dehumidifier.

To lower the temperature, increase the air flow in the grow room. This way you can help the warmer air out. We also recommend that you keep the lights off during the day and turn them on instead at night. You can also consider installing an air conditioning system, so as to also work on humidity.

To increase the humidity levels, you just need to get a spray of water: it is a manual solution that does not last long. So try to always keep the substrate wet (but not soaked). You can put open containers with water in your Grow Box.

To increase the temperature, you can install an electric heater, taking care not to heat the environment too much, ruining the whole crop. To optimize the heating process, you can insert a thermostat upstream of the stove or other heating device

CHAPTER 11

THE MOST COMMON SYSTEMS FOR HYDROPONIC CULTIVATION

Technological innovation has introduced unthinkable changes in agriculture in the last few years. One of these is the so-called hydroponic cultivation, a technique for growing plants without planting them in the ground outdoors.

Some call it hydroculture, due to the fundamental role that water plays. Others, more generally, indoor cultivation, to emphasize the indoor conduction of these crops, inside Grow Boxes or protected environments.

As we have seen, it is a cultivation technique that does not use the soil. The earth is a simple inert substrate (sand, clay, etc.) which serves to retain substances and minerals concentrated in a solution of water and nutrients.

No soil is required: this means that the crop does not consume soil, requires less space and does not necessarily require a fertile area to cultivate. It can be managed safely indoors, in small or very small spaces (even at home) and bears fruit even where the soil is poor or inhospitable for agriculture.

Plants grow faster. According to experts, hydroponic cultivation makes plants grow at least 20% faster than the soil, thanks to microprecision treatment with targeted doses of water, lighting and more (we will see in detail later).

The yields are higher: it is estimated from 20 to 25 percent more than cultivation on the ground, but a lot also depends on the technique and the art of those who manage it.

It saves a lot of water. Hydroponics slowly dispenses a little water per plant, without irrigating widely as in vegetable gardens or open fields. The water tanks are closed to prevent evaporation and adjusted to allow crops to absorb only the water they need.

Do-it-yourself hydroponics - cultivation techniques

Given the numerous ways to grow decorative plants or fruit and vegetables indoors with the hydroponic method, to decide the right one you will have to consider the space available, what you want to grow, how much it costs and how much time you can dedicate to it.

The three most recommended basic setups for beginners are:

The Wick system (with wick);

Water culture (hydroponics);

Ebb and flow.

All systems can be built starting from single components purchased separately, or through complete installation kits, online or in hydroponics stores.

Hydroponics with wick

The sprout of the plant is placed in a container with substrate (sand, gravel, perlite, etc.) and placed on top of a tank with water and nourishment. The container and tank are then connected with a wick of cloth or rope, immersed for one end in the ground and for the other soaked in water.

The capillary action of the fiber causes nutrient-filled water to rise to the growing medium, where it is absorbed by the plant roots.

Hydroponics dwc

The dwc (deep water culture) system is another extremely simple system, very suitable for plants that have a particular need for water (less so for long-lived ones).

In this case, the plants are placed on a polystyrene platform above a tank that contains the water and nutrient solution. A pneumatic air pump is then added to the black pot (isolated from light infiltrations), which, connected to the current, supplies oxygen to the roots of the plants.

Ebb and flow

A submersible pump and a timer regulate the flow of water and nourishment, which first invades the substrate where the roots rest and then is discharged back into the tank below.

This system allows you to further customize the crops we will see later as in a separate chapter.

CHAPTER 12
DEEP WATER CULTURE SYSTEM

Deepwater Culture hydroponics (also known as the raft system) places plant roots in a complete immersion of nutritious water. Within this raft-like system, plants float along in the water.

The depth of the water in the tank should vary between 8 and 25 cm deep for a complete suspension of plant origin in water and a nutrient solution. This depth also varies with the different sizes of the plants you are growing.

When fully submerged in a DWC bucket filled with well-oxygenated, nutrient-rich water throughout the day, crops rarely, if ever, endure nutrient deficiencies or a lack of appropriate oxygen for growth.

How does it work?

Hydroponic water heater systems allow the roots of small and large plants to thrive on nutritious water. There is a pump and an air stone under the tank to provide them with water for normal ingestion.

It needs a basic hydroponic setup to acquire this time-efficient method. As these roots remain underwater for life, they will constantly feed on the DWC stable nutrient flow method.

Don't forget to fill a sufficient amount of water in the tank that includes those plants. The water capacity of the container directly corresponds to the stability of the nutrient solution that the plants will receive.

All you need to do is keep an eye out for any accidental pump failure to avoid unwanted plant death.

WHAT DO I NEED TO ASSEMBLE A DWC?

As happens in almost all agricultural sectors, times have changed and DWC systems can also be conveniently purchased online through specialized shops. However, as mentioned above and given their relatively simple nature, these plants can easily be built with inexpensive materials. Basically, all you will need are:

A 13-22 liter bucket (for each plant)

A mesh pot that fits over the bucket lid (available from hydroponics stores)

An air pump and an "Air Stone" for aquaria

About 2 meters of 19mm silicone tubing

The substrate to put on the bottom of the net

1) The assembly is as simple as the materials used. The mesh pot is placed inside the bucket, making sure that the edges match perfectly with those of the bucket, in order to keep it raised. There must be a perfect fit between the two, in order to avoid accidents or

unexpected movements. At this point, we need to think about how to bring in oxygen. Make a small hole in the bottom of the bucket, just enough for the silicone tube to slide through. At one end you will connect your "Air Stone" (a small ventilation device made up of porous stones that will be placed on the bottom of the bucket) and at the other end, the air pump for aquaria. Be sure to place the pump higher than the bucket. In this way you will avoid, in the event of an interruption or shutdown, the water flowing in the opposite direction, damaging the pump.

2) Now, fill the water bucket with a small amount of water to test the aquarium pump. If air bubbles start to come out of the water then it means that we are ready to go! Fill the bucket with the nutrient solution until it reaches the top of the mesh pot above. This, in turn, will have previously been filled to the brim with your chosen growing medium. At this point you are ready to place the clone or seedling in the mesh pot. Sit back and relax. And here is a DWC hydroponic system unveiled! However, there are still some details to plan ...

3) To start this type of crop you will need a plant or a clone with developed roots. The choice is yours. To germinate seeds, we advise you to use rock wool cubes and, subsequently, move the seedlings that have developed into the mesh pot. The bucket will need to be cleaned and the nutrient solution changed once a week. This way you shouldn't have any problems keeping your plants healthy and strong all the time. Growing a plant by immersing its roots directly in a nutrient solution means constantly checking and adjusting the

pH levels.

WHAT ARE THE ADVANTAGES OF A DWC IMPLANT?

Over time, you will find that all of your initial expenses have been amortized. As you may have noticed in the previous guide, building this hydroponic system does not require any special skills or materials. Few accessories are needed, at least when growing few plants. A soil cultivation will never compete with a hydroponic cultivation, as the roots do not receive the same amount of oxygen as a constant flow of air. Furthermore, it is a system that can be extended. The principle is the same for growing multiple plants. If you decide to install multiple mesh pots, install a more powerful air pump to oxygenate a single large bucket or use multiple containers.

CHAPTER 13

WICK SYSTEM

Wick systems are easy to understand, simple in components, low maintenance, and inexpensive to build. Although still a part of hydroponic growing, they don't have any air pumps or stones. Eliminating these components makes wick systems the simplest form of hydroponic growing.

The whole concept of the wick system is based on capillary action - a process in which liquids travel against gravity through a piece of cloth or string. The plant regulates the force it takes to lift the solution from its roots, rather than the other way around.

Since it is the plant that is in the driver's seat, it will only extract the liquid it needs. The wick must be long enough to be immersed in the liquid solution, but also so that the other end makes contact with the root system of the plant. For topsoil: sand, gravel or perlite are all viable alternatives. Each can hold and absorb moisture. The exact type of substrate to choose depends on the effectiveness of your wick.

WICK HYDROPONIC SYSTEMS ARE A FANTASTIC SOLUTION FOR BEGINNERS

Wick systems eliminate several complications that can prove problematic for novice growers.

Not using soil is enough to remove the dangers of parasites, molds and other types of contamination. Using a wick provides a constant supply of nutrient-rich water. A beginner's tendency is to over-irrigate fearing that the plants are not getting enough water. Wick systems passively supply plants with only the water they need. These passive systems are silent and do not require electricity. Finally, although complete kits are available, a wick system can be built using easy-to-find materials. And thanks to the lack of moving parts, the danger of failure or breakage of the elements is practically non-existent.

BUILD YOUR WICK HYDROPONIC SYSTEM

Now let's go over how you can make your own. A quick note before we delve into the details: the most crucial aspect to consider is the quality of your wick. It is, after all, the core part of any wick hydroponic system. The material of your wick will directly determine the rate and amount of liquid it is capable of absorbing and carrying to your plant.

Everyday household items that can be used as a wick are nylon cords, floor mop cords, strips of old clothes, and strips of plastic. Before using them you can test each of these materials with colored water. After at least an hour you should have some indication of how high and fast the water is flowing. Finally, for best results, use two wicks per plant.

Wick system

INSTRUCTIONS

Fill a jar or small bucket with nutrient-rich water. Ideally, the container should be slightly smaller in circumference than your grow pot, and opaque. The container will act as a reservoir.

Take the pot you intend to use for your plant and place both wicks in the center. There must be a small hole in the bottom of the pot so that the wicks can pass.

Fill the pot with growing medium, making sure the wicks are long enough to make contact with your plant's root system and are submerged in the nutrient solution.

The wick length may need some adjustment. Place the plant pot over the container from step one. The pot containing the plant must now be suspended above the water, with the wicks partially submerged.

To prevent any pests or contamination, make sure the tank is sealed.

DISADVANTAGES

Despite its simplicity, this method is not without flaws and limitations, such as:

Not suitable for large and very thirsty plants

The growing medium can hold nutrients, causing a build-up of toxic substances

The water in the tank can become stagnant

Mold can develop if the system is not cleaned regularly

If the tank is sealed, providing oxygen to the roots can be a problem

The solution should be regularly tested to verify the correct pH value

One piece of equipment that can nullify some of the disadvantages is a pump attached to an air stone. This will provide oxygen to the water and prevent the accumulation of waterborne diseases. However, this system increases the initial cost and requires you to have your wick system close to a power source. Inserting a pump therefore makes the whole system no longer passive.

Using a hydroponic wick system is a tempting prospect. A significant amount of complications are taken away from the novice grower. Unfortunately, wick systems are easy to build, but difficult to master.

The material and length of the wick, the amount of solution and the frequency of refilling, all these factors are unknown until you start using it and experimenting with this growing method. They are ideal for a few home-grown plants. Given the minimal cost of building a wick system, what is there to lose?

CHAPTER 14
EBB AND FLOW SYSTEM

E bb and flow hydroponic systems are particularly recommended for inexperienced growers.

EBB & FLOW methods are a great choice for novice growers, as their elements are simple to use and have neither excessive volume nor excessive potency.

The techniques of Ebb and Flow in hydroponic cultivation allow you to regularly check the parameters and results of the growth of your plants, ensuring the maximum yield and quality of your production.

HOW EBB AND FLOW HYDROPONIC SYSTEMS WORK

These systems are widely used for hydroponic cultivation and particularly suitable for indoor crops.

An EBB & FLOW hydroponic system consists of a single cultivation tray, in which two different types of substrate are placed, to be chosen from:

Expanded clay;

Sand.

The plants of the crop are then placed in the tray. Alternatively, the substrate can also be placed in pots already positioned directly in the system.

At the base of the tray, the nutrient solution is added or poured, which is absorbed by the plants thanks to a good oxygenation system, guaranteed by the components of the hydroponic system.

To insert the nutrients simply pour them in to fill the tray and then empty it. The results are also excellent in the case of cultivation from seed to the point that this method is particularly effective, unlike other types of hydroponic cultivation.

Furthermore, the operation of Ebb & Flow is quite simple. This makes it almost as used as the drip hydroponic system. Let's find out what its advantages are.

ADVANTAGES OF AN EBB AND FLOW SYSTEM

These hydroponic systems guarantee effectiveness and efficiency for the success of your crops.

For example, the method of water outflow from the plant area is very important because it avoids creating excessive accumulations of nutrients or obstructions of the system components. This way the plants are not harmed.

Benefits

Excellent plant re- oxygenation function;

Small footprint;

Silent system;

Economic;

Ease of programming.

Ebb-flow systems, also called tidal hydroponic systems, also require simple hydroponics equipment, consisting of accessories such as a tray, rubber hoses, timer-controlled water pumps and a tank with lid.

This hydroponic cultivation system involves the use of two containers, one that will house the plants and one that will contain the nutrient solution.

The substantial difference is the use of a pump and a timer that allows to program the spraying, which is generally evaluated according to the needs and the type of substrate used.

The container with the solution is placed at the bottom and is connected to that of the plants placed at the top by means of a tube or a duct that will allow the pumped solution to return to spray the roots in the starting container by gravity.

This continuous circulation sprays and nourishes the plants and oxygenates the water in an excellent way and all autonomously, with the help of a simple pump that pushes the nutrient solution towards the roots of the plants.

The container for the plants is generally square or rectangular in shape and the plants supported by an inert substrate such as rock wool, coir or expanded clay.

Having learned the basic concept of active hydroponic systems, which has the aid of a pump that circulates the nutrient solution, we will be able to learn more about the various types in use today and the types of substrate used, but we will also distinguish hydroponics from aeroponics. Then, the various components that can integrate the various systems, starting from various types of pumps, lamps that reproduce the action of the sun, the hydroponic greenhouse or Grow Box, air filtering systems and all the automation systems, up to the self-powered electrical and heating systems of hydroponics and everything we need to build and manage the well-known DIY hydroponic system / hydroponic system, and enter the world of do-it-yourself hydroponic agriculture or hydroculture.

CHAPTER 15
THE NUTRITIVE FILM TECHNIQUE

HYDROPONIC SYSTEMS WITH NUTRITIONAL FILM AND NUTRITIONAL FLOW

Active hydroponic systems: nft systems, (Nutrient Film Technique) with nutritive film, innovation and yield enclosed in a simple and ingenious system.

Among the cheapest hydroponic systems to build.

These hydroponic systems have become very popular due to their simplicity of construction and care, and the low cost of the materials is suitable for crops with a short vegetative cycle such as salads, and various types of vegetables.

The system consists of a series of inclined channels on which the drilled pots with plants are inserted, generally supported by rock wool or other inert material.

It is not suitable for the maintenance of very large plants with a long life cycle as the same conformation of the system does not allow the plants to anchor firmly, therefore they will be subject to sagging, which can be partially resolved with a support grid made with simple threads for agriculture as in the greenhouse cultivation of tomatoes.

A pump introduces the nutrient solution into the channel which, due to the effect of gravity, flows, wetting and nourishing the plants and then enters the subsequent channels and continues its work until it returns to the storage tank.

The channels have the characteristic of having a flat and wide bottom, and a maximum height of about 5 cm, this allows the solution to flow forming a film like a flowing river.

In this way, just as happens in nature for streams and rivers, the oxygen contained in the air mixes and dissolves in the solution, oxygenating it, thus allowing the plants to live.

NFT HYDROPONIC SYSTEMS

Indoor cultivation

This hydroponic technique, like other indoor cultivation techniques, is not without drawbacks. Unfortunately, the shape of the channels does not allow a large accumulation of nutrient solution which, during normal operation is its strong point, but if a failure should occur at the pump, the plants would have a few hours to live, especially if this happened on a hot summer day.

To solve this problem, the system has relatively evolved into the DFT hydroponic or nutrient flow system in which the channels are placed on the level, and are divided into various sections with small internal bulkheads, and the nutrient solution is then transshipped to the next section and so on.

But this system also has its drawbacks.

First of all the channels have greater depth, for the realization of the bulkheads and this means having to germinate the seedlings and make sure that the roots are long enough to reach the nutrient solution before introducing them into the system as well as in case of pump or other failure, the plants would only have a few more hours of life.

In both systems, only one pump is used, in my opinion to solve the problem it is enough to use two independent pumps that do the same job so that in the event of one failure, the other will continue to feed the plants, then if they both break ... .

Before spending hundreds of euros on a ready-made system, you can build a DIY nft hydroponics system with materials that are easily available in hardware stores, grow shops and online.

CHAPTER 16

PUMP SYSTEMS

CLOSED-CYCLE HYDROPONIC SYSTEMS, AN INNOVATION IN HYDROPONIC CULTURE THAT COMBINES THE STRENGTH OF WATER AND AIR TO FEED THE VEGETABLES IN SYNERGY.

One of the hydroponic cultivation systems that are still widely used today, was put in place in the eighties by Lawrence Brooke. This simple but effective system is composed of a bifurcated tube that allows the air blown at one end to push towards the plants and oxygenate the nutrient solution.

It is used instead of the liquid pump, a sort of compressor that generates air flow which, when introduced into the device, meets the column of nutrient solution and pushes it out, oxygenating it.

The air enters from the small tube which then travels upwards, mixed with the nutrient solution.

These systems consist of two pots, one with a hole that contains the plant and which allows the solution to flow towards the second pot which acts as a container for the nutrient solution and as a support for the first pot.

A hydroponic system of this type is very suitable for very large pints with a long life cycle, a sort of hydroponic pot.

VORTEX or Hillel vortex system, hydroponics without pump.

Hydroponic agriculture with the vortex hydroponic system. The vortex system exploits the rotation of a hollow cone, such as a funnel which, by rotating, generates the movement of water forming a vortex.

The nutrient solution that rotates collects kinetic energy directed towards the outside of the cone and, finding the inclined surface of the cone itself, goes up, the only possible way, splashing towards the roots of the plants and feeding them.

As for Lawrence Brooke, the Vortex system also consists of two pots, one with a hole that contains the plant and which allows the solution to flow towards the second pot, which acts as a container for the nutrient solution and as a support for the first pot and also houses the immersion motor, equipped with an impeller cone for spraying the nutritive solution.

Both systems are very efficient, especially in very hot places, thanks to the cooling action of the air which becomes saturated with water vapor, thus creating an environment particularly suitable for survival.

These hydroponic systems are often mistakenly referred to as aeroponic systems, but as we have seen, aeroponics is a completely different type of indoor cultivation.

CHAPTER 17

DRIP SYSTEM

D rip hydroponics developed at the same time as NFT and DFT hydroponics.

The same structure for these hydroponic crops can be used the same as the NFT hydroponic system, formed by slightly inclined channels that allow the nutrient solution to flow towards the storage tank or simply plastic trays on which to place the rock wool or coconut fiber substrate.

The plants are housed in the channels by means of special mesh jars typical of hydroponics, supported by a substrate of rock wool or coconut fiber and are sprayed by a drip system, as in land-based agriculture.

In the case of the seeds, on the other hand, they are simply placed in the trays with the substrate.

The pump pushes the nutrient solution into a main tube from which the capillary tubes branch off and reach each single plant, nourishing it drop by drop, hence the name of the system.

The substrate

The fiber substrate receives the water and releases it very slowly, while in the meantime the roots absorb the nutrients they need.

In most of these hydroculture systems, the solution administered to the plants and not absorbed, is about 35% is, with consequent economic expenditure and environmental damage, so if you approach this type of system, take care at least to still use the excess solution to feed other plants, perhaps the ornamental plants you have in pots or those you have in the garden.

Apart from this small drawback, the drip system offers many advantages, in recent years other types of 100% biodegradable substrate such as glass wool and coir have been introduced.

The fiberglass substrate protects the root from sudden changes in temperature, helping the less experienced grower.

But above all, the system is essentially composed of a tray, a pump and tubes for irrigation, all materials that are easily found and at low cost, therefore excellent for those who want to try for the first time to build a hydroponic farming system at home.

CHAPTER 18

HOW TO BUILD A DO IT YOURSELF

SYSTEM

A bout 300 plants in 6 square meters? It is no longer science fiction, with vertical hydroponics systems it is possible!

Vertical hydroponics systems are capable of optimizing space efficiently, exploiting height instead of width.

These systems have been designed in order to grow plants, indoor crops without soil.

Indoor cultivation, both for the success and for the ease of execution by enthusiasts and professionals in the sector, have meant that do-it-yourself hydroponics systems expanded and found more and more fans.

Today, hydroponic cultivation is quietly practiced at home, in the garden, and on the roofs of disused structures.

Between technique, art, and do-it-yourself, let's see how to build a hydroponic system.

Hydroponics systems: how to build one

Building hydroponics systems without buying ready-made

systems represents a hobby as well as a way to economize, and to optimize available space.

The first thing to do is to understand which system you want to build, what to buy, in terms of tools and accessories, and then go into the actual construction of a hydroponic system step by step.

Very high quality, excellent results and savings will be the objectives to keep in mind.

The hydroponic systems that can be built are varied, and the difficulties of construction and set-up are different, without forgetting that different systems satisfy different needs.

In general, to simplify, we can say that to create a hydroponic system you need plastic bags (one with a capacity of 5/10 liters and one of 4/9 liters), a suitable substrate to be used in hydroponics, an oxygenator and an immersion pump.

Continuing, I still need plastic containers, such as glasses and / or small jars, pipes with specific characteristics for irrigation and a timer.

The function of the timer is to allow the planning and subsequent dispensing of the nutrient solution, since it is a soilless system, remember that it must also be fed.

The necessary items vary according to the type of plants you want to grow, the space available, etc.

For those who are not used to it, do not worry: a little commitment, a lot of will and above all manual skills are enough.

For the realization of a simplified hydroponics system, that is, the one that consists of plastic bags, substrate, oxygenator pump, 2 plastic containers (resistant plastic cups), watering pipes and timer, the only tool to buy is the submersible pump.

The pump must develop a power of 4/30 W, which is necessary so that the power of the jet is not too high. For buckets, large plastic paint buckets are fine (we recommend that they be properly cleaned), another fundamental thing is that one of the two buckets is smaller than the other, so that it can fit in the other.

Furthermore, the two buckets must not be transparent, they must not filter the light inside the vase, if in doubt, a safe coat of paint will solve the problem.

With a drill, you need to make holes in the smaller bucket. It must be filled with expanded clay, one made up of typical porous pebbles, very light, similar to pumice stone.

The larger bucket must be filled with at least 4 liters of water, then the pump must be immersed, inserting the oxygenation tube in the appropriate space.

In order not to damage the pump, the watering pipes must be connected, thus avoiding immersing it completely in water.

The cups must be placed in the bucket filled with expanded clay, after drilling them to allow the future development of the roots.

Even the glasses should be properly filled with clay. At the end of this last operation, you can proceed to fit the smaller bucket inside the larger one.

During the interlocking operation of the two buckets, care must be taken in order to make the watering pipes come out and connect them to the highest bucket, right above the cups.

The tubes must be fixed at a height of 5/10 cm from the cups and be supported on the vase, to ensure greater fixing, block them with wire.

First connect the pump to a timer and then to an electrical outlet, in order to obtain an automated system.

The pots must be of smaller and smaller diameter, in order to let the water fall onto the underlying pot, it does not matter what materials they are made of, it matters that they are dark, to avoid the passage of light.

A final precaution is to make the hydroponic plants grow in the expanded clay, facilitating germination.

CHAPTER 19

FERTILIZERS

Hydroponic cultivation is undoubtedly one of the most innovative and efficient techniques for gardening and indoor vegetable gardening. Thanks to its simple operating principles, it is possible to create a green corner in any room of the house.

But for the maintenance of a perfect small indoor garden it is necessary to use fertilizing solutions to constantly and in the right way, feed your decorative seedlings or vegetables. In addition to mineral or chemical fertilizers, there are various products on the market, of organic origin, suitable for every type of plant and vegetative phase.

Whichever crop you choose for hydroponics, there are several fertilizers that provide your plants with the right nutrition.

As for plants grown on the ground, even for those grown soilless, the right amount of mineral salts and nutritional elements is essential.

The main ones are:

nitrogen;

phosphorus;

potassium;

calcium;

magnesium.

These elements (or rather, macro elements) must not be missing during the vegetative and development phases of the plant. These nutrients, then, must be accompanied by other necessary nutritional elements (called microelements), which vary according to the type of plant and the growth phase in which it is found:

manganese;

iron;

sulfur;

zinc;

boron;

molybdenum.

In hydroponic cultivation, all the nutrients, which the soil usually releases spontaneously, must be controlled and managed manually in the correct way. It is an operation that may seem complex to beginners, but, with the right guidance, the management of a hydroponic mini - soil can become very simple and intuitive. On the market there are nutritional solutions to be dissolved in water, in the right quantity and according to the doses indicated on the product label.

The advantages of fertilizers

Fertilizers for the hydroponic system provide the macro and microelements useful for growing plants in an optimal way during each of their vegetative phases.

Among the different products commercially available for hydroponic cultivation, there are several compounds that stimulate the germination of seeds and the rooting of cuttings in coconut fiber and other substrates.

There are different types of fertilizers which, in general, must be diluted in water and placed in the irrigation system of hydroponic greenhouses. The best nutritional solution should be chosen based on the type of plant and its vegetative phase.

In decorative plants with inflorescence, fertilizers with low nitrogen and high potassium content increase the production and quality of the flowers.

The hydroponic cultivation technique is increasingly widespread, not only in agriculture, but also in private homes, where it is not always possible to have a small garden or a vegetable garden on the balcony, due to its many advantages: the versatility of the system; the excellent results in the production of inflorescences; the absence of pests and diseases related to the exposure of plants to the outside air; the economy and simplicity of system management. Without the constraint of seasonality, then, it is possible to have available all year round, vegetables typical of the summer season (such as tomatoes, zucchini, eggplant, etc.), immediately ready for consumption and with genuine flavor.

With the hydroponic system therefore, it is possible to take advantage of any environment or small space in the house and create a small green oasis, full of scents, colors, fruits and vegetables to be consumed fresh and to be used in the kitchen. But to get the most out of your hydroponic mini - soil it is necessary to keep some fundamental factors under control:

lighting;

temperature;

humidity rate;

circulation;

presence of the right amount of fertilizers;

pH and EC level (electrical conductivity, used to determine the salinity of the nutritional solution, ie the quantity of dissolved salts) of the substrate.

All of these factors are crucial to keeping your plants healthy and avoiding the formation of mold or mildew. In particular, then, taking care to administer the right dose of nutrient solution, at the correct time, is of vital importance for the growth and well-being of all plants.

And precisely for a correct use of fertilizers, there are some useful precautions to be observed.

First of all, remember that the fertilizer solution must be administered in different dosages according to the vegetative phase of the plant.

The nutrient solution to be administered to the plants must always be diluted in water and introduced into the irrigation system, so that it is distributed evenly in the substrate. You can use running tap water, as long as it is of good quality.

Also, remember to observe the doses indicated on the label or suggested by your trusted nurseryman: an excessive amount of fertilizer, just like an insufficient amount, risks irreparably damaging your plants.

Check pH and EC values of the substrate at regular intervals, which may be subject to fluctuations.

CHAPTER 20
VERTICAL HYDROPONICS

Vertical hydroponics, the evolution of indoor cultivation that makes the most of space and maximizes the yield of cultivation.

With the emergence of hydroponics in industrial production, much attention has been paid to yield, to obtain ever higher profits for the same space used.

This is how vertical systems began, which replaced the traditional horizontal systems.

Vertical cultivation, as the term indicates, develops in height, to raise the cultivation density of plants per square meter.

There are several types, the main ones are as follows.

With an inverted V-shaped frame on which the channels are mounted that will contain the plants that will be sprayed with the nutrient solution by means of sprayers or another chosen system.

Vertical frame, formed by long sacks filled with laterite or expanded clay on which the plant feed is inserted by pumping the solution into the upper part of the sack and it wets the roots, nourishing the plants while flowing downwards

Vertical cylinder in which the plants are anchored to a cylinder placed vertically with the roots outwards, each equipped with a bag containing the substrate that will be sprayed with the nutrient solution by means of drippers.

Advantages of vertical growers

The vertical cylinder system offers the advantage of being able to position the lighting directly in the center of it and therefore to provide the plants with direct light and not reflected on the reflecting panels.

Another system that can increase the cultivation density is the rotary cylinder system, structurally the same as the vertical cylinder, with the plants anchored on the perimeter of the cylinder with the root facing outwards, wrapped in a bag containing the substrate, and the lighting placed in the center.

With the difference that the cylinder is placed horizontally and rested on rollers mounted on a frame with a tank of nutrient solution underneath.

The cylinder is made to rotate by means of a motor so that the roots are immersed in the solution at each rotation.

All these systems are obviously suitable for plants with a short life cycle and with a reduced volume for the simple fact that if they grew a lot in volume, they would take light and air from each other.

These hydroculture systems are in fact mainly used for the cultivation of lettuce, radicchio, endive, aromatic plants and all short cycle and reduced volume plants.

CHAPTER 21

PH CONTROL AND MAINTENANCE FOR HYDROPONIC CULTIVATION

What is pH?

The pH value provides a measure of the acidity or alkalinity of an aqueous solution and is proportional to the concentration of hydrogen ions. The measurement scale goes from 0 to 14, a neutral solution has a value equal to 7, an acid solution has a value less than 7 and an alkaline solution has a value greater than 7.

pH for nutrient solutions

A correct pH value allows plants to absorb the right nutrients for lush growth. The right pH value for your plants should be between 5.5 and 6.3. High pH values above 6.5 and below 4.5-5.0 are to be avoided. The precise pH value that determines the precipitation of macro-nutrients is due to the combined concentrations of calcium and sulphate. A fertilizer containing a high content of calcium and sulfate, the solution will need to be kept at a pH plus step. If the pH of the solution is too high, greater than 6.5 there is a risk of a precipitation of salts that would be missing from the plant and would clog the irrigation system.

Adjustment of the pH

Remember to check the pH of the solution:

1. When adding nutrients to the solution.

2. After adding water to the solution.

3. In recirculation systems, the pH must be checked on a daily basis because the absorption of water and nutrients by the plants causes the change in pH.

If the pH of the solution remains high for too long, the precipitate of the salts cannot be dissolved again and the solution must be changed urgently.

To minimize pH fluctuations it is recommended to:

1. Use branded pH stable fertilizers

2. Provide at least 9/10 liters of solution for each large plant, below this quantity there is a risk of an excessive pH variation due to possible variations in heat / cold due to evaporation.

3. Try to keep the grow room temperature below 30°C and humidity above 50%.

PH adjustment steps:

Measure pH: use a liquid pH indicator, or an electronic pH meter. Before measuring the pH, make sure the fertilizer is well mixed and the sample container is clean.

If the pH tends to increase continuously (the most common trend), it is recommended at each adjustment to reduce the pH to

88

about 5.0. This will give you a more adequate "safety" margin than an initial pH of 5.8.

If the pH tends to decrease constantly, it is advisable to increase the pH to about 6.0 in each adjustment.

pH Adjustment: add a small amount of pH - / pH +. Mix well and check the pH. Repeat this process until the target pH is reached.

pH measurement with "pH-meters"

A pH meter is the right tool to measure the pH of your solution. There are many very reliable and cheap electronic pH meters on the market (these pH meters need to be calibrated and cleaned).

It is not recommended to use pH meters for swimming pools or aquaria because most of the time the measurement scale stops at 6.0.

pH tests, have a reagent that is mixed with the solution you want to test and reacts by giving a color to the solution. This color will have to be compared on a scale of values, so each color will have a different value.

Before measuring the pH make sure that the nutrients or the pH - or pH + added to the solution have been mixed properly.

CONTROL AND MEASUREMENT OF THE CONDUCTIVITY OF NUTRITIONAL SOLUTIONS

What is the conductivity of a solution?

A conductivity meter, or EC meter (also known as "MS", "CF" or "TDS ") is a device used to help monitor the concentration of nutrient solutions.

'Conductivity' represents the ease with which a solution conducts electricity. Numerically it is measured in units called Siemens. Solid matter known as 'salts' (eg sodium chloride, potassium nitrate), release ions when dissolved in water. The ions allow electricity to flow through the solution.

Liquids such as gasoline and pure water are essentially non-conductive of electricity.

Factors affecting the EC value

The concentration of a salt in solution is understood as the quantity present. With relatively dilute solutions of soluble salts (i.e. up to 100 ppm or so), if the concentration doubles, its conductivity also doubles. At higher concentrations however, this strict proportionality (IE linearity) deteriorates.

Note: there is a better linear relationship between concentration and conductivity at low values 1-2 g / L compared to 10 and 20 g / L.

The effect of temperature on the conductivity of the solution is such that its value increases by approximately 2% for each 1°C increase. The conductivity of a solution varies according to the type of salt present and is determined by factors such as the 'size' of ions, and the 'charge density' of the same.

Purchase of a conductivity meter

The following specifications are important to help you purchase a good EC Meter:

Possibility of producing readings also in Siemens (for example, "MS") or CF and not only with yield in TDS (ppm).

Calibration: EC meter with the possibility of calibration (automatic if possible). It helps to ensure maximum precision even when the electrodes are not performing to original specifications for example, electrode due to contamination, physical damage, etc.

Possibly waterproof and floats - helps protect against injury / mistreatment.

That it has temperature compensation: an integrated temperature sensor allows you to adjust the meter to view the readings what it would be if the temperature was at 25°C / 77°F.

Long battery life - with auto power off function to extend battery life.

Conclusion - conductivity and hydroponics

Since nutrient mixes in hydroponics are usually composed entirely of salts, their approximate concentration can be determined from their conductivity (EC) values. However, as discussed above, because each individual nutrient has its own (i.e. different) specific conductivity value, and since, in a hydroponic system, the concentration ratios between nutrients are constantly changing, careful interpretation needs to be given to the reading of the conductivity values. Only large differences in conductivity value found on a day-to-day basis can have meaning.

However, despite some difficulties, if used with intelligence, the conductivity value is a precious control aid for an excellent cultivation success.

The pH measures the "potential of hydrogen" therefore the relative concentration of positive and negative ions in the water.

The greater the concentration of negative ions compared to the positive ions and the greater the acidity of the water, vice versa the greater the concentration of positive ions compared to the negative ions, the lower the acidity of the water.

As this ratio varies, therefore, the water will be more or less acidic depending on the concentration of a certain type of ionic charge.

For example:

a pH of 0, therefore acid, is that of battery acid in which the positive ions are 1×10^0 and the negative ions 1×10^{14}.

A pH of 14, therefore alkaline, is the lye in which the positive ions are 1×10^{14} and the negative ions 1×10^0.

A pH of 7, therefore a neutral pH, is that of pure water in which the positive ions are 1×10^0 and the negative ions are 1×10^0, therefore they are equivalent.

Obviously the thing is much more complex, but this is enough to have an idea of what we are going to act on.

Moving on to practice, each type of cultivation needs a very precise pH, so in order to make the nutrient solution suitable for the cultivation it is intended for, first of all, measurements must be made.

Different types of tests are available on the market to carry out the measurements.

Litmus papers, strips of paper impregnated with litmus, a substance composed of various dyes obtained from certain types of lichens which reacts to the substances in which it is soaked, taking on different colors depending on the acidity of the liquid itself. Usually the numerical value of the pH with respect to the color is reported on the appropriate pH table.

Reagents, liquid or powder substances that when immersed in the liquid to be tested take on a different color, to which a numerical value is assigned.

Once the pH value of the nutrient solution in question has been established, the value will be corrected if necessary with an additive with the right characteristics

If the pH is too high or too low, additives can be used which, added to the solution, lower or raise the pH value, depending on the product used and the amount of nutrient solution to be treated, the right dose of additive will be added. A few seconds will change the values.

All additives are sold in all grow shops and stores dedicated to this type of indoor cultivation.

CHAPTER 22
SUBSTRATES

Hydroponic cultivation has come a long way in recent times given the growing interest in obtaining controlled production throughout the year, even in adverse climatic conditions and without the problem of unsuitable soils for crops, such as rocky or sandy ones.

Hydroponic cultivation allows crops to be controlled both from a qualitative point of view and from compliance with hygiene and health standards, an increasingly important issue these days.

Hydroponic growing is a type of indoor growing, meaning it can be started inside a greenhouse or in your own home. To start this type of cultivation on a large scale, it is necessary to have adequate structures, have access to suitable energy sources, and obtain substrates.

The substrate: what it is

Hydroponic farming takes place out of the ground. The earth is replaced by a mixed layer, which is made of various materials, mixed together, mixed with sand or used alone. The most common are for example clay, coconut fiber, and rock wool.

This mixed layer made with various materials is none other than the substrate that is the protagonist of our article, the characteristics of which we will soon go into.

The substrate takes care of absorbing all the substances useful for plant growth. In its absence, the cultivation is carried out exclusively through water. The substrate is sown and the plants are grown.

The substrate: characteristics

Hydroponic cultivation solves the problem of soil not being suitable for growing the crop optimally, thanks to the substrate, which we have said is a mixed layer made of various materials.

The substrate deals with the absorption of nutrients useful for plant growth, does not require fertilizers or herbicides and sees little use for pesticides. However, the substrate needs irrigation with a nutrient solution.

Better substrates

What are the best substrates for hydroponic growing? Certainly, rock wool, a soft and permeable material, with low water retention and great ability to circulate oxygen. Rock wool is therefore optimal for preserving plant photosynthesis.

Then there is peat, a soft organic substance perfect for receiving plant roots. However, it must always be kept moist so it needs constant control.

Expanded clay is excellent, it has great water retention and high draining power. Expanded clay can be reused for many other crops and is easily sterilized. Surely it is perhaps the best substrate for hydroponics among all.

Another very good substrate for hydroponic cultivation is vermiculite, an inorganic material used for drainage. Vermiculite can be mixed with portions of sand, is lightweight and is generally sold in bags.

Mainly the choice must be made on the basis of a mechanical requirement, in the sense that based on the development that the plant is expected to have, the material that will support the weight of the same will be chosen.

Essentially, any type of substrate could be used in a hydroponic system as long as it allows the root to absorb nutrients, in fact the main success factor of hydroponics is the spraying of the roots.

It is necessary to allow time for the nutrient solution administered to drain and at the same time make sure that the substrate itself is never too dry.

In some cases, only for purely aesthetic reasons, substrates similar to soil are chosen, such as coconut fiber that hides the roots, while in others it is chosen to cultivate with the roots exposed, immersed directly in the nutrient solution.

They are mainly divided into organic substrates and inorganic substrates.

The main characteristics that a good substrate must possess are:

Porosity, which can be up to three times higher than that of the soil, which allows the roots to make their way effortlessly with a significant positive impetus for growth.

Drainage; a substrate can be even 100 times more draining than a common soil, this allows the roots to always be in contact with mineral salts and various nutrients, facilitating the growth of the plant.

These two factors determine water retention and water potential.

Water retention is the amount of water that a given amount of substrate can absorb.

The water potential represents the strength with which the substrate retains water and is measured in kPa, "kilo pascal".

These two factors are essential and must be balanced with the spraying of nutrient solution in order to keep the substrate wet at the right point.

It should also be chosen with a water potential suitable for the type of root it will host as if the water potential is greater than the force that the root is able to exert to absorb nutrients, it will eventually die.

CHAPTER 23
ENLIGHTENMENT

Hydroponic lamps are the same for indoor growing. These lamps are used to replace naturally occurring sunlight. Many hydroponic systems are used in greenhouses or indoors and therefore artificial light is vital.

The lamps for growing in hydroponics differ between models and power.

Here is a list of the most common

HPS -MH: gas discharge lamps that require a ballast for ignition. They are among the most used because they have excellent efficiency.

CFL: low consumption lamps, excellent for energy saving and low heat emission, however they are also low penetration.

LED: LED panels are a new innovative lighting source that is giving excellent results even if they are perhaps still a little too expensive.

In fact, there is little to say, without light the plants die, and with poor light they do not grow or struggle to grow, so it is important to offer more than adequate artificial lighting that resembles the much loved sun as much as possible.

Therefore, knowing how to choose the right lamps to offer good lighting in indoor cultivation of all plants is a more than fundamental factor. In fact, it is extremely important to make the right choices regarding lighting because this will surely be one of the most important "investments" of all cultivation.

To start, we can say that the most widespread and used lamps for lighting in indoor cultivation are divided into three main types:

Low consumption CFL lamps

HID lamps for cultivation

Led lamps for indoor cultivation

Low consumption CFL lamps

CFL: Compact Fluorescent Lights are nothing more than the classic low consumption fluorescent lamps that you have surely installed at home too. They are extremely cheap, are found everywhere and also offer an excellent yield for the growth of our plants. The lamps generally come with a standard E27 socket and it is therefore possible to insert them in numerous lamp holders. But let's see the pros and cons of this type of lamp:

For

Availability and low price. You can buy them in hardware stores, in any lighting shop, but also in simple "everything for the home" shops, so really everywhere; also, all at a much lower price compared to competing lamps. To this we can then add excellent light output and a wide range of different types, such as the "daylight" (daylight - cold) of 6400-6500k of white / bluish color, ideal for the vegetative phase or the "warm 2700k white" (warm light) with a redder light spectrum ideal for flowering.

Against

They have lower light intensity compared to their competitors, this means that more lamps have to be installed for each number of plants or m3, which is obviously not an important factor for small crops; secondly, they tend to heat up, so it is not possible to place them too close to the plants and raise the temperature of the whole environment (but this could also be seen as a Pro in certain situations).

Since indoor cultivation will generally only take the vegetative phase of the plants and therefore the flowering phase will be carried out outdoors, I recommend the purchase of only "daylight" lamps, therefore cold light 6400-6500k and with as many lumens (luminous flux) as possible. Generally being quite long, it is natural to put them horizontally; in this way, however, half of the light emission will be lost, so I recommend using a special reflector to solve the problem.

Important: There are specific CFL lamps for indoor cultivation, these offer better performance in terms of light output and temperatures; of course, being specific and better, they have a higher price and are sold only in specialized stores for cultivation and online. However, I recommend that you take them into consideration for a possible purchase.

HID lamps for cultivation

HID (High Intensity Discharge) are one of the most used types in indoor cultivation, especially in the cannabis sector, but they are perfect for all crops.

There are the bulbs: MH (Metal Halide) and HPS (High Pressure Sodium). The main difference between the two is that MH emits a "colder" and bluish light and is therefore ideal for the vegetative growth phase, while HPS emit a "warmer" and reddish light, and is therefore ideal for the flowering phase.

For

They are quite cheap compared to other lighting systems, they are easy to install but above all they are a very reliable solution for obtaining excellent results. In fact, with a basic kit for less than 100 euros you can have a complete 600w lamp that, in addition to cultivating, you can safely use to tan.

Against

The lamps emit a large amount of heat, so a good ventilation system must be combined to better ventilate and refresh the environment. They also have a very limited duration, in fact over time their luminous intensity tends to decrease and therefore you will have to change them quite often, usually every year. Another con is the plug. In fact they do not provide a standard one but need a special power supply (as already mentioned there are ready-to-use kits) and furthermore their luminous power requires a considerable energy demand, therefore electricity bills will be high.

Also for these, like the previous ones, since they will only be used for the vegetative phase I recommend only the purchase of the MH cold light type, generally with power from 600w upwards. If you want to grow completely indoors, you can opt to buy both lamps, and change them for the various stages.

LED lamps for indoor cultivation

In recent years, LED lights have really made great strides in the lighting sector, in fact just think that until a few years ago they were not recommended for use in indoor cultivation, while now they are one of the main alternatives.

In fact, modern LED lights emit an exceptional quantity of lumens per Watt and thanks to the new COP (Chips on Board) technology they emit and supply a light intensity suited to the needs of the plants, with incredible light penetration. We can therefore say that today LED lights can equal or even surpass the lamps illustrated above from multiple points of view. But let's analyze the Pros and Cons:

For

They are absolutely the best solution for indoor growing in terms of energy efficiency and low power consumption. Another important factor is the almost absence of heat emission (unlike the previous lamps) and the functionality of having a classic socket without purchasing special power supplies such as HID, and perhaps most importantly: they have an infinite duration.

Against

For LEDs, I don't think there are any real cons, apart from the price. In fact from a technical point of view they are absolutely the best solution, but it must be said that a serious basic LED system, specific for cultivation, has a cost of a few hundred euros and therefore are not really within everyone's reach, but of course there are cheaper solutions that can be adopted.

How to choose LED lamps

Unfortunately, being a recent technology that is still continuing to develop, it is difficult to say precisely how and which lamps to buy, in fact, while the previous types of lamps now are standardized, the LEDs improve every year from every point of view, so what can be the best LED product this year may already become "obsolete" next year.

To save money, you can adopt LED solutions for the home (such as light bulbs or strips) or cheaper technologies (usually Chinese) which have a good quality / price ratio and offer good results. Of course, being cheaper they are also less efficient, but personally I managed to get good results even with these while staying on a rather low budget.

Plasma lamps (LEP)

Plasma lamps are one of the best performing indoor lighting solutions ever, but also the most expensive. These use a technology based on fused quartz plasma cells containing a special gas and other particular substances. The operation takes place with a heating of the bulb through a discharge of microwaves (radiation) that allow it to be switched on and therefore emit light. With this technology we therefore have a lamp without electrical connection and therefore without wear and tear. The light produced by this lamp is full spectrum, almost identical to that of the sun and therefore ideal for any plant phase. Of course we are talking about lamps with a retail price above a thousand euros!

High efficiency CMH lamps (LEC)

LEC (Light Emitting Ceramic) use particular bulbs called CMH (Ceramin Metal Halide), which are nothing more than an evolution of the already mentioned and most used HID lamps. Unlike the latter, however, the LECs are able to emit a higher color temperature of light, almost equaling that of the sun (Sun: CRI 100, Lec: CRI 80-96). Thanks to this technology, the lamp is able to have a more complete light spectrum with balanced UV levels almost similar to the plasma lamps mentioned above. Typically, with a base lamp with a 315w and 3100°K bulb, about 36,000 lumens are produced with a perfect spectrum for all plant phases. This type of lamp is cheaper than the previous ones, with a retail price of around 400 euros per lamp.

Neon lamps

Another lighting technology used in cultivation is neon. There is little to say about these lamps, I believe that anyone who has a neon ceiling light in their house or garage knows they are very economical both in purchase price and in management and consumption, and they also offer good results. With this technology it is possible to use the classic indoor or outdoor neon ceiling lights used at home, but there are also specific solutions for cultivation that are quite cheap (less than 100 euros for a complete professional lamp) with greater light output and reflectors that direct light better.

Which type of lamps to choose?

Unfortunately, answering this question is not very simple, because the choice may be due to many factors such as the quantity of plants, the total space, the equipment placed side by side (heating-ventilation), the budget and much more; but by calculating a classic cultivation situation as a hobby or for a small business (thus leaving aside the LEP and LEC lamps which are very expensive and therefore for purely professional and large-scale use), surely the best solution is to make a small investment for LED lamps as they offer excellent lighting, perfect for cultivation, but above all they have a long life and consume little electricity. Of course, as already mentioned, for this technology it is also possible to opt for cheaper solutions by spending a few tens of euros and still having excellent results, thus leaving out the more expensive professional systems.

You could consider CFL lamps, as they are very cheap and above all they are found everywhere; and once the Grow Box has been disassembled, it is possible to use them safely for the home, for the garden or for the garage, without leaving them unused in a corner.

HID lamps, as they have quite high operating costs, heat a lot, and therefore also need good ventilation so as not to raise the ambient temperature too much.

Of course, as far as possible, I highly recommend doing it yourself for the entire system, buying cable by the meter, single connections and bulbs and mounting everything as you wish; so as to save money and have a perfect solution for your needs.

For my Grow Box, for example, I personally created a system by assembling different components and putting LED lamps for a total of 30,000 lumens with a very limited consumption.

Calculate the amount of light for indoor growing.

The unit of measurement for the illuminance is the Lux (lx), which is equal to one Lumen (lm) divided by one square meter (m2). The minimum required to grow plants correctly is 21,000 Lux; to make you understand better you must know that the sunlight on average varies between 32,000 and 100,000 lux.

Therefore you need to know:

How big in cubic meters (m3) is your box or the space dedicated to plants.

How many lumens can your lighting system generate (always check this value before buying a lamp).

With these two data in hand, all you have to do is divide the total number of lumens that your lighting system develops divided by the volume of your box in m3 and you will have the actual number of lux that your system can generate.

Attention: We said that lux are Lumens per m2, and why are we now talking about m3?

Because simply the height at which we will position our lamps is fundamental for an exact data of the light that will illuminate our Grow Box. In fact, on a certain area, if we place a lamp at 50 cm or at 2 meters, the final result will be very different; because the higher the lamp is raised, the more the light beam tends to widen, losing intensity.

So based on this we have slightly adapted the mathematical formula for what we need specifically.

But let's take a practical example to better understand how to calculate.

I'll give you a quick calculation with the dimensions of a hypothetical Grow Box of 125x50x50 cm, I multiply these values and they give me the volume: 312,500 cm3, I transform the cm3 into m3 and I get 0.312 m3, this is the actual volume of my box.

Now I calculate the lumens of my lighting system: assuming that I have a led system made up of two 5,000 lumen lamps, I will have a total of 10,000 lumens.

Now just divide the number of lumens by the m3 of the box, so: 10,000 lm / 0.312 m3 = 32,051 lux.

So I managed to create a lighting system in a box that generates 32,051 lux. Looking at what was said before, we are therefore well above the minimum values for a correct indoor cultivation.

My advice is to always stay above the minimum recommended value, therefore to be around the minimum value of the sun, therefore above 30,000 lux, so as to offer correct lighting to the plants.

I recommend that you always make this calculation before buying the lamps, so as to evaluate in advance whether a particular lamp can be useful or not, without wasting money.

NB: if you do not use a Grow Box and you grow your plants in an open space, you will naturally have a dispersion of light, so I advise you to put some reflectors in order to direct all the light downwards.

Once you have created the perfect setup to offer excellent light output to your plants, remember to offer the maximum "dose" of light in the growth phase by simulating that it is always the longest day of the year (21 June) and therefore with over 15 hours of light per day (16-18 hours of continuous light is a good solution).

How do I know when the light output is ideal?

It will be the plants who tell you. If they stay low and grow in width and thickness of the stem, then the light is perfect, if instead they tend to "spin" (stretching) therefore remaining slender and growing only in height, it means that they are looking for light and therefore the light output is too low and you will have to either bring the lamps closer or increase the power. If they tend to soften or even burn, the lamps are probably too close or too powerful and therefore you will have to move them away; (in this case you can let the plants rest in the dark for a few days and then put them back into the light with the right setting).

I recommend connecting the lighting system to a socket with a built-in timer, so as to have fully automatic switching on and off even when you are away from home.

CHAPTER 24

GERMINATION TECHNIQUES

How to prepare cubes for indoor germination: all types and techniques

Germination is the first of the three stages of a plant's life cycle. The other two are Growth and Bloom. It is an evolution process that begins when there is an environment with ideal humidity and temperature for the seed. In practice, the seeds begin to absorb water and this makes them grow in size causing the fabric to break and open. In a nutshell, to simplify, the seed opens and the root comes out, indispensable for the survival of the plant itself and is source of supplying the nutrients that the plant needs.

To germinate the seeds, three typical tools of hydroponic cultivation are essential:

Mini greenhouse (in which to germinate the seeds)

Rock wool cubes (at least 1 for each seed you want to germinate)

Root stimulator (the fertilizer)

These three tools are essential for germination and must be used with care as seed germination is a delicate moment in the plant's life cycle.

Start with the mini greenhouse

In summary, for germination you need a controlled environment, where there is adequate temperature and humidity: ie, the mini greenhouse where you can insert the seeds to germinate or the containers for sowing.

Each seed is inserted into a single cube of rock wool. Finally, add a root stimulator which in practice is a typical fertilizer or nourishment in the hydroponic technique.

In this section we explain how to germinate seeds to get sprouts and start indoor cultivation. To properly prepare the germination area you need to have:

Cubes or discs for germination

A stimulator to quickly develop the root system of the plants

Germination in rock wool cubes

To prepare the germination area it is necessary to have cubes of rock wool and the root booster, in order to quickly develop the root system of the plants.

Below we illustrate the characteristics and the procedure to start - step by step - the germination phase in rock wool cubes.

Prepare a solution with 5 liters of water and 20 ml of root stimulator.

Take the rock wool cubes and soak them for about 24 hours in the stimulator water solution to make the rock wool cubes less alkaline (their pH tends to 7.0).

The following day, drain the cubes. The cubes hold a lot of water, so it is useful to drain them, to allow a correct exchange of water and oxygen.

Insert the seed into the hole (of the cube) to a depth of 5mm.

Insert the cubes inside the mini-soil and keep the temperature at about 25/26°C with high humidity (about 80%).

Bring the neon lamp closer and keep it on 24 hours a day (until the plant starts to come out).

The seed does not initially need too strong a light. Once the plant has come out of the cube, it is however essential to illuminate with delicate light (better if you use a neon type light, or HPS and / or MH lamp (monitoring temperature and humidity). Depending on the type, quality and age of the seeds, germination can take from 2 to 14 days.

The roots, once out of the cube, will tend to protrude from the sides and bottom of the cube itself. The seed in the germination phase is very delicate and must not be touched.

Germination in peat or coconut discs

Prepare a solution of water and root stimulator.

The Jiffy disk must be placed in a basin with two fingers of solution for about twenty minutes so that it swells completely and becomes a cylinder about 5 cm high.

Insert the seed into the hole provided on the upper side of the disc.

The disk can be moved and completely buried in the cultivation substrate.

Below we illustrate the procedure for successfully germinating in peat and coco cubes.

Prepare a solution of water and root stimulator.

Moisten the cube with the solution, it must be neither too dry nor too wet.

Insert the seed in the center of the hole 5mm below the surface.

Insert the cubes inside the mini -soil and keep the temperature at about 25/26°C with high humidity (about 80%).

Bring the germination lamp closer and keep it on for 24 hours a day.

The seed - in its first phase - does not need light. Once the plant has come out of the cube, however, it is essential to illuminate with a delicate blue or white light (preferably neon) or with MH growth lamps (monitoring temperature and humidity). Seedlings that do not receive adequate light tend to have very long (stretching) stems. Depending on the type, quality and age of the seeds, germination can take from 2 to 14 days.

6 tricks to remember

1. Choose the method that best suits your type of cultivation

There are several techniques for germinating seeds - if you plan on using a hydroponics system, rock wool or Root Riot cubes are the ideal choice. If you will be growing in potting soil or coir, you can use Jiffy discs and then switch to a small pot with lightly fertilized soil.

2. Plant more seeds than you need

Not all seeds germinate, so it's recommended to germinate more seeds than you need in case. If all the seeds planted do germinate, you will have a bigger harvest

3. Pre-soaking of seeds

This is optional, but if you choose to soak the seeds for at least 6 hours and no more than 12, you have the option of placing the slightly hatched and "softened" seed directly into the cube or directly into the soil. In this way you will speed up the process of hatching the seed and further speeding the seeds by at least 2 days.

The water used must be at room temperature and very small doses of stimulators can be added to favor germination.

4. Keep humidity and temperature constant

There are many propagators to choose from, each suited to a different environment. For the winter climate a heated propagator could be the best choice, this helps to reach the necessary temperature and humidity. For hot weather, unheated plastic locks can also be used. It is highly recommended to nebulize the water also in the internal part of the propagator, this favors the right level of humidity.

5. Correct lighting

To aid the germination process of the seeds, it is advisable to use lights with a cold - blue color spectrum such as CFL bulbs or neon tubes. These lamps produce little heat and can be placed close to plants to maximize the light they receive. Keep the HPS for later!

6. Have Patience!

Don't try to transplant plants too early. Some seeds show signs of growth in less than 24 hours, others may take 3-4 days or more just to come out of the cube. It can be tempting to transplant as soon as the plants open their first leaves, but the wait will reward the grower! By maintaining high humidity (80-100%) and stable temperatures between 21°C and 26°C, your seedlings will be ready for transplanting after 10-28 days (depending on the seed). In 10-28 days, most plants have developed a strong root system and are ready to start the vegetative growth phase

CHAPTER 25

TO HAVE HEALTHY PLANTS BEWARE
OF FUNGI

Roots are not usually given due attention. This statement is true whatever the chosen cultivation method is, but even more so for the hydroponic one, since the roots are sterile and vulnerable. Therefore, when choosing hydroponics, the discussion of root care is extremely important.

But don't the roots take care of themselves? Generally, yes, but.... If they find themselves in adverse situations, they are easy prey to various diseases. A good grower must prevent the problem before it occurs. The question is how to keep the root system healthy.

In hydroponic cultivation the main ingredients of success are: a dynamic and well-designed cultivation system; clean and highly oxygenated water; a well-watered substrate; good ventilation and adequate levels of temperature and humidity. Of course, there are many other parameters to take into consideration, but if you follow these basic guidelines and the usage tables on the nutrient bottles, you will be able to keep your plants happy and healthy. And, ultimately, that's exactly what you want, because insects and diseases start invading a plant when it is stressed.

The root is a particularly vulnerable part of the plant, whether grown in soil or in water. If the temperature is high and the water circulation is poor, your plants suffer from a lack of oxygen. At the root level, this lack of oxygen reduces the permeability of the roots to water and consequently also the absorption of mineral salts, which will lead to a weakening of the plant and, finally, to a poor harvest. If the plant is subjected to persistent conditions of stress, the roots produce ethylene, a stress hormone that accumulates in the roots and participates in the slow degradation of the root system. Additionally, some pathogens recognize ethylene as a sign of plant weakness and a reason to attack.

What is a pathogen?

It is an organism that causes disease. There are many of them, among which we find mushrooms such as Fusarium and Pythium. Fusarium and Pythium are the most common and destructive root attackers known to both hydroponic and soil growers. These very ferocious invaders are often the cause of the total destruction of a crop.

What is Pythium?

Pythium is a destructive root parasitic fungus. Under suitable conditions, Pythium multiplies very quickly and frees microscopic spores that infect the root and deprive the plant of its nourishment. It mainly attacks seeds and seedlings, which offer less resistance to disease. Larger plants are more resistant but can still be attacked with the difference that, if you can detect the pathogen quickly, they can be cured and saved, even if your yield will still be poor. Like other fungi, Pythium can be present in any part of the plant and attacks practically all varieties. The best conditions for its development are high levels of humidity and a temperature between 20 and 30 degrees, as well as poor oxygenation of nutrients in the case of hydroponic cultivation. It is a fungal spore that lives in the air and water and is present in the growing area, even if you always keep it clean. It gets onto your shoes, clothes, hands, etc. It ends up in your water, especially when it comes from wells, rivers or streams. There are millions of opportunities for this mushroom to enter your garden. It is therefore important to keep your growing environment clean and to try to understand where the water you use comes from.

Pythium is often identified as a "secondary infection" since it attacks the plant only when it has already started to suffer damage or when growing conditions are not the best. It takes advantage of diseased or injured tissue to colonize the root and create leaking or root rot.

How to recognize a Pythium attack

Generally, when Pythium attacks, the infected seeds become soft, mushy and black, after which they die. The stems become weak. The larger plants and the mothers begin to wilt and turn yellow for no apparent reason (for this reason the process is erroneously referred to as nutrient deficiency) and sometimes the leaves tend to curl downwards. The plants show poor growth and the yield is reduced. Total loss of the crop can also occur.

It is not easy to catch a Pythium attack in time.

If you're not vigilant enough, the consequences can be dire.

If you look at the roots when Pythium has already started attacking your plants, you may notice different symptoms, depending on the extent of the damage. The infection starts from the extremity of the root and then slowly disintegrates the lateral roots, very important for the absorption of nutrients. The bright white of the roots changes first to light brown, then to dark brown and finally to black. When the infection is acute, the lower part of the stem can become sticky and black. Generally, it is possible to separate the rotten part of the root, which goes from the soft to the sticky, from the innermost part.

How to fight Pythium

The answer is quite simple: by keeping your plants healthy, you will allow them to resist fungal attacks. In hydroponics, there are some basic and mandatory rules to keep plants healthy, namely good quality water, excellent oxygenation of the nutrient solution, good ventilation, a well-sprayed substrate, adequate levels of temperature and humidity, suitable nutrition and general cleansing. These are the essential preventative measures that all hydroponics growers should always keep in mind, as prevention remains the most effective weapon.

1. Check the seedlings closely, as it is usually at this stage that the plants are attacked. It is important to choose the germination substrate very carefully and to keep the germination area as clean as possible.

2. Always keep the environment as clean as possible.

3. In principle, start with disease-free plants and seeds. Avoid overfeeding and crowding plants and maintain good ventilation. It seems that Pythium thrives best in the presence of high levels of alkalinity, so try to keep the pH of your plants as low as possible while always trying to satisfy the plant's needs.

There are other methods to prevent Pythium and other fungi in general. Some companies offer products such as special silicate powders, beneficial bacteria or fungi, or mixtures of various species of both. Others still go further and offer a "bacterial filter" that filters all residues, increases the oxygenation of the water and includes a mixture of microorganisms which, once colonized, form a protective barrier on the roots, thus blocking the invasion of pathogens. For this filter to work well it is necessary to keep the roots healthy, even if you cannot keep the temperature levels under control.

CHAPTER 26

HOW TO GROW BASIL AND ROSEMARY

Basil and Rosemary: grow them in water to keep them fresh whenever you want.

Basil

To start hydroponics with basil you can use seeds, which will be germinated. The second method is faster and generally more successful: it usually takes a week for the roots to sprout in water.

It is important to remember to keep the temperature between 21 and 26 degrees Celsius, since basil loves heat but not excessive heat. In the pots you can insert the rock wool cubes, which are the favorites for this cultivation. Otherwise, sphagnum, perlite, vermiculite or coconut fiber can also be used. All these will still need to be sterilized before being used. In addition, make sure that the substrate in which to grow the plants is always only moist and not too wet, otherwise harmful fungi can develop.

It is possible to harvest basil when the plant is at least 20 cm high and always only by cutting a third or maximum two thirds of the branch. However, after you have already cut each branch two or three times it is advisable to start the cultivation again with new cuttings.

Rosemary

The hydroculture of rosemary is slower: you have to wait at least 12 weeks before you can harvest a few twigs, while if you start from the seeds it takes even longer and the chances of harvesting are even lower.

Rosemary can also be attacked by fungi, powdery mildew and mites: for this reason, it is one of the plants for which hydroponics with the NFT system (Nutrient Film Technique) is recommended. Furthermore:

The pH must remain between 5.5 and 7.0

The humidity level must not rise too high

At least 11 hours of sunlight a day must be ensured

Harvesting can take place all year round, but for each plant it is always good not to go beyond two or three times.

CHAPTER 27

GROWING TOMATOES

How to grow tomatoes

The tomato is the prince of summer vegetables: with its aroma, color and intense flavor, it is the main ingredient of many tasty, light and healthy recipes.

Rich in vitamins and antioxidants, it is a panacea for our health.

With the hydroponic growing system, it is possible to grow this vegetable at home and benefit from its fruits all year round. A few tricks are enough to obtain great results and enjoy fresh tomatoes, excellent to be savored raw in salads, or to make fragrant sauces for first courses.

Although originally from Central and South America, the tomato has been one of the most cultivated vegetables in the Mediterranean for more than a millennium.

In fact, in this geographical area, this fruit has found the ideal environment and climate to grow and develop in all its many varieties.

Eaten raw, in sauces, or cooked, tomatoes are the fundamental ingredient of many summer recipes, but it is also a panacea for our body: low-calorie, rich in vitamins, minerals and substances with important antioxidant properties.

Tomatoes have a taste that is appreciated by adults and children, and varies in the different types, from a more acidulous and fresh taste, to a sweeter one, like that of datterini.

Which tomato varieties can be grown at home?

The tomato is a typically summer vegetable: if grown outdoors, sowing and transplanting the seedlings should generally be done in spring.

Clearly, with the hydroponic mini - soil, cultivation is no longer affected by the season!

The plant adapts easily to different space requirements, so you can also plant it in pots on the balcony, grow it on the terrace, or indoors with the hydroponic system.

The most suitable varieties for home cultivation are those with smaller fruits, often used for sauces with basil, but also excellent to be eaten fresh in salads.

Cherry (also known as pachino tomato)

Datterino

Mini San Marzano

The tomato, as mentioned, is a typically summer vegetable. If you choose indoor hydroponic cultivation, you can enjoy its fruits even in the winter.

The hydroponic greenhouse, in fact, even in agriculture on a commercial scale, has proved to be a successful technique for the cultivation of many vegetables, and tomatoes in particular.

Hydroponics is able to respond in a more than satisfactory way to all the needs of the plant: from nourishment, to exposure, to climatic conditions.

The substrate guarantees the tomato the ideal type of support for root growth and plant development, in a growing environment in which certain conditions are met:

Constant humidity and water drainage;

Oxygenation of the roots;

Right amount of nutrients;

Environment free of pests and molds.

Before starting tomato cultivation, it is necessary to prepare the substrate with the most suitable fertilizers that release the nutrients that the vegetables need to germinate, grow and produce the vegetables. The tomato, in particular, also needs good quantities of nitrogen, phosphorus and potassium. Ask the nurseryman, to ensure proper fertigation for your plants.

In the indoor garden with hydroponics, you can recreate the ideal conditions for germination, growth and fruit production by setting the temperature and lighting of the greenhouse to reproduce spring and summer climate.

Tomato seedlings need air to grow and develop, so it is necessary to maintain an adequate distance between the seedlings and eliminate excess leaves as the vegetables grow.

To get the best results from your indoor tomato garden, you need to keep in mind some notions about the growth and development of this type of plant.

You can plant the seeds, or transplant the seedlings into the substrate.

Keep a distance of at least 12 cm between one plant and another for the "dwarf varieties" and at least 25 cm for the other varieties. If necessary, place braces to support the vertically growing stems.

The hydroponic greenhouse must guarantee some fundamental parameters:

Temperature around 22-25°C;

Humidity without stagnation of water;

Constant lighting for 16-18 hours a day;

pH values between 5.5-6.5;

Nutrition suitable for the needs of the crop.

The seedlings should be irrigated with frequent watering, more abundantly during fruit production, but it is important that the substrate drains the excess liquid to avoid root rot which would be fatal for the whole crop.

About 10 weeks after germination, the tomatoes are ripe and ready for harvesting. To keep production constant and profitable, the bulky leaves under the ripening bunch must be removed periodically. Another fundamental operation is that of leaf removal, that is the pruning of the so-called "axillary buds" (also called female) that grow on the stem of the plant, without being productive and with the direct consequence of depriving it of the resources necessary for its growth. Especially in indoor cultivation, it is advisable to also top the plants and keep the height of the plants under control.

Although hydroponic cultivation guarantees conditions in which plants are less subject to attack by parasites, the tomato is subject to the attack of insects and diseases that arise with excess humidity.

Always pay the utmost attention to the appearance of the plants and their fruits, keep the cultivation parameters in balance and intervene promptly in case of alterations or diseases.

The hydroponic garden is the ideal solution for those who love summer vegetables and decide to dedicate a space at home to the cultivation of these precious "golden apples". An original idea is to combine the cultivation of tomatoes with basil and rocket, but also edible flowers and summer vegetables. These plant species, in fact, get along well both in the garden and on the plate.

CHAPTER 28
GROWING PEPPERS WITH
HYDROPONICS

Hydroponic peppers are more advanced than tomatoes and lettuce. With the correct hydroponic method, pepper cultivation will lead to better results than many ground-grown pepper plants.

Grow the healthiest plants in ideal conditions of temperature, light, pH level, etc., to achieve optimal pepper production and flowering of pepper seedlings. Growers like you will have excellent yields with this hydroponic pepper grower.

How To Select The Varieties Of Peppers?

There is a large selection of pepper plant species on the market for successful home gardening. But hydroponic growers will have a hard time choosing the right strain for this particular method.

It depends on your tastes and your prerequisites. You can also opt for a mixture of colors starting from pepper seeds, with red and green peppers at the same time.

Which Hydroponic System Works Best For Peppers?

The weight of adult hydroponic peppers determines the

appropriate hydroponic system. With vigorous pepper growth, some constructions may not be able to handle their good-sized veggies.

For this reason, the system should provide sufficient support for these crops. It's best to find out more about the size of your pepper variety before deciding on any version.

Apart from popular systems such as the nutrient film technique, the wick system or the drip system, deep water culture, Ebb and flow are the most suitable methods for hydroponic peppers.

It doesn't matter if you are a home gardener or a commercial grower. These low-cost hydraulic mechanisms automatically provide an adequate irrigation solution and oxygenated nutrition.

Ideal conditions for hydroponic peppers

Humidity

The humidity required to grow peppers in hydroponics ranges from 55 to 65 percent. A higher percentage can lead can lead to deformed fruit.

It is okay to develop this plant within an environment such as a conventional tunnel or under a shade cloth. However, it will not be easy to maintain the ideal size throughout its development.

pH

One of the most essential aspects of hydroponic gardening is the pH level. When this rate is too low or too high, the expanding pepper plant will fail to efficiently ingest important water minerals.

The best pH for peppers in a hydroponic environment is between 6.0 and 6.5. Make sure that pH fluctuations do not occur on a regular basis to preserve plant growth at a steady pace and with adequate pH.

Raising peppers requires at least 14-18 hours of light per day for stable development.

Although some artificial lights such as fluorescent ones may not be intense, you can use a HID or LED grow light that also works well for your indoor plant heating system. Commercial growers will prefer this type of lighting.

Also, my advice is to continually raise the delicate rack higher as those plants thrive for a perfect 6" space between them. This measurement will produce adequate but not excessively strong direct illumination.

Temperature

There is a particular guideline regarding temperature range for pepper development that every gardener strictly follows. Night temperatures should be above 18°C and around 30°C during the day.

You will need to keep the growing temperature below 34°C. Even in warm temperatures, it should never reach 35°C to prevent the flowers from falling off.

Remember that the temperature can affect the total development of the pepper. A sudden change in this factor will reduce the quality of the fruit, so maintaining a balance is crucial.

Nutrition

To provide the plant with the nutrients for hydroponic peppers, it is necessary to use a nutrient program that promotes vegetative growth. A one-component nutrient solution is a perfect choice for pepper preparation.

When it has reached the flowering stage, reduce the nitrogen and switch to some other one-component nutrient product.

Depending on your chosen regimen, you can add dietary supplements to further nourish the nutritious plants.

Plant Spacing

Regular spacing of pepper plants is important for full development. It is necessary to arrange a distance of 18 to 61 cm between the plants for the best conditions.

You can put them closer than this distance, but there is a potential risk of reduced lighting. Nearby peppers can prevent some of their components from receiving proper light treatment.

How To Prune And Harvest Peppers

You shouldn't allow hydroponic peppers to reach their full height without any intervention. At about 20 cm in height, then, it is necessary to start pruning and pinching the plant to spur its development.

The action of pruning sweet pepper plants prevents them from growing too large. The ripening time varies between 50 and 90 days.

Also, many types of peppers have an early green phase, but they can turn yellow, reddish, even purple as they grow. Therefore, it will be worth waiting to harvest these plants some time later.

CHAPTER 29

HOW TO GROW LETTUCE

Growing salad in hydroponics is extremely simple, simpler than it might seem; even for those starting from scratch and approaching the world of hydroponics for the first time. First of all, it should be noted that to grow the salad with this system it is possible to use any system: the drip system, the Ebb & flow system and the NFT system.

After talking about the hydroponic garden, let's now see how lettuce is in reality the simplest thing to grow, so it is the most suitable type of product for those who are trying their hand at indoor cultivation for the first time.

Once you have identified the variety of salad that best suits your needs and tastes, you have to get the seeds, which you can find online or buy them directly in one of the grow shops in your city, then you will have to buy rock wool cubes and mesh jars, mini-soil to store them warm, in a protected environment and mesh jars, designed specifically for the needs of plants that are grown with hydroponic and aeroponic systems. Therefore, a small hydroponic or aeroponic system will be needed.

So let's see the steps to take.

The salad seeds are placed inside the rock wool cubes, moistened (it is recommended not to insert more than five seeds in each cube) only with water and then placed inside the mini-soil , at a temperature between 23 and 28 degrees centigrade.

One aspect to check - when using rock wool cubes - is the amount of water they absorb, because an excessive amount of liquid could lead to root rot and drowning. For this reason, it is always advisable to check the levels of liquid present and possibly squeeze the cubes to release excess water.

With the right amount of water and the ideal temperature, lettuce seeds will start germinating after about 48 hours. When you see the first roots sprout from the rock wool cubes (both from the sides and from the base), it means that the time has come to transfer the newly born seedlings into the special mesh pots, which will first be filled with expanded clay and then settle them into the hydroponic system of your choice (or aeroponic). The seedlings inserted in the aeroponic system will then be fed with a special nutrient solution based on water and fertilizers in order to provide everything they need. It is important to avoid any type of fertilizer during the germination phase and then start with half the dosage recommended on the package.

Fertilizers

By using suitable fertilizers and in the right dose, the roots of lettuce seedlings are allowed to develop better and faster than they would with a traditional cultivation system, also because - in this way - the roots are able to receive and assimilate nutrients more quickly.

To make the seedlings grow in a healthy and fast way, thus also strengthening their root system in order to make it more robust, it is possible to opt for some particular fertilizers, which contain fundamental substances capable of promoting and increasing growth, accelerating absorption of nutrients, and keep common diseases away.

Fertilizers play a fundamental role in the life and health of the plant.

Hydroponic salad: parameters to monitor

At this point, once the cultivation has started, it is advisable to keep under control some important values for the health and growth of each plant, such as the pH, which will determine the plant's to correctly absorb the available nutrients. To ensure that the salad plants absorb all the nutrients correctly, the pH must be slightly acidic and to ensure that it is always so, it is advisable to monitor the situation often with manual tests. Use the paper strips for the pH test, they are the most economical and easy to use.

Tips and Tricks for a perfect hydroponic salad

To create a suitable and protected environment, it is advisable to repair and check salad plants inside a Grow Box, in order to make them grow well, healthily and faster, without costing more.

Among the advantages of using the Grow Box there is that of

being able to control the temperature more easily than in a larger environment and, therefore, better manage the ventilation, ensure the right lighting (thanks to the reflective mylar sheet present inside the Grow Box that allows the light to be propagated effectively).

But when will the first salad crop be obtained?

Much depends on the variety chosen and grown, but - in general - it is possible to say that the time required varies between 28 and 80 days. By choosing different varieties and managing the aeroponic system as best you can, you can have fresh, tasty and healthy salad at any time of the year.

Growing the salad indoors allows you to manage the environment and prolong the harvest.

To help growth, it is advisable to properly illuminate the salad plants: the best solution is to use HID discharge lamps or with LEDs, but you can also find a good compromise by using fluorescent lamps. To better manage the lighting of the salad plants, it is advisable to activate the lights for 12 hours a day, thus guaranteeing 12 hours of darkness.

For starters, it is wise to purchase a simple lighting set consisting of 4 CFL lamps, enough for a home grow.

CHAPTER 30

HOW TO GROW PARSLEY

B efore planting parsley, pre -sowing preparation should be done. Since the seeds of a crop sprout for a long time, gardeners have resorted to methods of accelerating growth. For this, bubbling is used - oxygen treatment of seeds. To do this, they are placed in prepared water and stirred periodically.

It is important that the oxygen is evenly distributed over the entire thickness of the seed.

First sow dried parsley seeds in the open air. However, they must not be exposed to direct sunlight.

When the installation is ready, the plant container is filled with the substrate. It is a sterile substance that does not contain any components. The substrate must not be affected by humidity and other substances. It serves as a support for the root system.

You can prepare a solution for hydroponics yourself. In this case it is important that the water that will be used for its preparation does not contain foreign substances. To prepare the solution, water-soluble fertilizers are used which contain trace elements necessary for the development of vegetation. The concentration of salts in them should not exceed 3g per liter of water, otherwise the plants will die from dehydration. As a rule, gardeners buy a ready-made solution in specialized stores.

Parsley seeds are sown in a prepared substrate at the rate of 1g per 1 m2. After planting, the site is watered abundantly to provide the amount of moisture required for germination. In the water used for irrigation it is recommended to dissolve special fertilizers, or agents of similar composition. After watering, the containers with planted seeds are covered with foil, this will create a greenhouse effect. When parsley is grown cyclically, the next sowing is done after 2 weeks.

If parsley is grown in a greenhouse, drip irrigation is used after the emergence of the sprouts. That is, they provide water supply to each individual plant. The drip irrigation system supplies water to the root system through drippers and pipes. This method of irrigation is quite beneficial for gardeners, as it reduces the cost of stimulants and fertilizers, and also reduces labor costs.

Note! While growing parsley, neither drying out nor excessive moisture should be allowed. Watering is done every week. Otherwise, the leaves and roots of plants will not be able to absorb the required amount of nutrients, which will lead to various diseases.

Optimal humidity mode:

90-100% - in the first days of sowing;

60-80% - 2 weeks after sowing.

The film will help maintain high humidity in the first few days.

The optimum temperature for growing parsley should not be below 14 degrees, the substrate temperature should not be below 3 degrees.

Deviations in temperature and humidity from the corresponding standards prevent normal plant growth and increase the risk of developing diseases.

Parasites and diseases

Most often, parsley is vulnerable to powdery mildew. The main signs of this disease are the formation of a white bloom on the leaves and the slowing of the growth of vegetation. Such bushes should be immediately uprooted and thrown away from the other plants. After 2 leaves appear on the plants, they can be treated with fungicides.

Aphids cause serious damage to the crop, at any stage of growth. Pests feed on plant sap, as a result of which the leaves curl and dry out.

Collection

How much parsley is grown hydroponically? It is harvested after 5 weeks. The upper part of the leaves is simply cut off. The shoots remain for continuous growth. If the seeds have gone through bubbling before planting, the harvest time will speed up significantly.

Cleaning the equipment

After harvesting the parsley, the equipment must be disinfected. After removing the solution, the system is thoroughly cleaned of plant residues. To wash the equipment, an irrigation system is used, and hydrogen peroxide is used. During the cleaning process, change the water at least 2 times. It is recommended to rinse the substrate (especially coconut) with boiling water, this will destroy all bacteria and fungi. Then it is air dried.

CHAPTER 31
PRACTICAL ADVICE

L et's recap the phases of hydroponic cultivation

Step 1 - Prepare well for hydroponic cultivation

We prepare the seeds

First, take a kitchen glass or a coffee cup, fill it with tap water and soak the seeds in it for 24 hours.

This promotes the hydration of the seed and activates the germination hormone as well as softening the cuticle (peel) of the seed and thus allowing better germination. The plant can use less force to be able to break the shell (less stress) and you will get plants that are very close to each other (homogeneous germination).

Let's get the rock wool ready

We immerse the rock wool cubes in a container with water adjusted to pH 5.5 for 24h.

Contrary to popular belief, this step is essential for two reasons.

It allows the water that passes through the rock wool to remain at the same pH and does not undergo variations that could raise or lower the entire pH of our tank (nutrient solution), and the seedling from the first phase of life will grow with the perfect pH value to fully assimilate all the nutrients of our solution.

Take a pH meter, calibrate it and adjust the pH of the water to 5.5. Then dip in all the cubes you need for the number of plants you want to grow (3 rock wools = 3 plants).

We prepare the clay

Now we just have to prepare the last fundamental component of our hydroponic system. Half fill a large basin with water and pour a few drops of hydrogen peroxide into it to disinfect it, then put the clay in it.

Thanks to this step you will eliminate the sand present in the middle of the clay, which could clog the hydroponic system and you will disinfect it from possible bacteria that could proliferate inside the water.

Take a vase from your hydroponic system and fill it to the brim with clay, pour the clay into the basin and repeat this step for the number of vessels in your system (if my system houses 10 vessels I will repeat the operation 10 times).

This means that you can calculate the right amount of clay to fill all the vessels in the system, since we will have to calibrate and rinse it before inserting it into the system itself. We calibrate the water in the basin at a pH lower than 4.5 and let it rest for 24 hours.

Thus the water that will pass through the middle of the clay in the future does not undergo pH variations , which could modify the entire pH of the solution present in the tank.

The roots that expand, enveloping the clay, will find an environment with a perfect pH to absorb all the nutrients of the system.

We take our clay after 24 hours and rinse it under running tap water, to completely eliminate all residues. We are ready to fill our jars!

Step 2 - Commissioning of the Hydroponics System

At this point we have everything you need to put our hydroponic cultivation system into operation, ready to give you great satisfaction and above all heavy harvests! Follow these tips to start immediately at the top!

Step 1/5 - How much water is in my system?

In all hydroponic systems the total capacity of the tank is indicated in the user manual, obviously the one indicated is the maximum capacity, so we should insert less water than that shown in the booklet.

If you have a small hydroponics system (4-8 plants) insert 10 liters less than the capacity indicated in the manual.

If you have a large hydroponic system (over 10 pots) add 15 liters less than the maximum capacity.

At this point you also need to know that to fill your system you have to use a certain type of water:

65% Tap water;

35% Osmotic water (distilled).

Otherwise you can fill the whole system with 100% Osmotic Water.

To fill the system, I mainly use 30l of water which I divide into 10 liters of osmotic water (which I get using my reverse osmosis filter) and 20 liters of tap water. The water must have a temperature of between 18-24°C, so that the roots remain well oxygenated.

Before putting water into your system, please read step 2 below.

Step 2/5 - Preparation of nutrients and pH

After we have filled a 20l tank of tap water and 10l of osmotic water (if you use a system that holds 30l) before pouring the tanks into the system, we need to adjust the amount of fertilizers and the pH.

Following the diagram that indicates the recommended amount for each week of growth (expressed in ml), I notice that I have to pour 2.5 ml for every 10 liters of water. I then calculate 2.5 x 3 = 7.5ml (since I have 30 liters in the tank) and then I administer nourishment to the tanks before pouring them so that I can adjust the pH before putting them into the hydroponic system.

To distribute the nourishment in the 2 tanks, I put 5ml in the 20l tank and 2.5ml in the 10l one (2.5ml every 10 liters). Now I shake the tanks to distribute the fertilizer evenly in the water and wait 2 minutes (the fertilizer lowers the pH of the water).

I measure the pH with the pH tester and add the pH- until a value of 5.5 - 5.8 is obtained. Now we can pour the tanks with the nutrients into the hydroponic system, every time we change the water to the system we will use this system by first putting the fertilizer in and adjusting the pH before pouring the solution in.

Tip: it is always good practice to make a mark to indicate the water level when the system contains exactly the liters you have chosen to use so you can monitor when the water level begins to drop.

Step 3/5 - Let's time our system

We pour the water into the system and operate the pump, every time we change the water we make the pump work for at least an hour in order to distribute the new nourishment to our plants. Now we just have to set the timer to time the operation of the pump and the irrigation of the system.

There are 2 schemes to follow:

Until the roots of the plants reach the water present inside the tank (if you use a system similar to mine) we have to make the timer work in steps of 15 minutes every hour (we lower 1 peg of the timer every hour). We must keep this programming even when our lamps are off or during the night.

The roots are immersed in the water of the system: we maintain 15 minutes of irrigation every hour during the period of light (lamps on). We will run 30 minutes of irrigation only in the middle of the dark period so if our dark period lasts 6 hours we will run 30 minutes of irrigation after 3 hours. If our dark period lasts 12 hours, we will run the system after 6 hours of darkness for 30 minutes.

If the system you use is different, and the roots of the plant do not touch the water of the reservoirs, run it 15 minutes every hour, both during the period of light and during the period of darkness.

Step 4/5 - Weekly addition of hydroponic liquid fertilizer

Follow this program if you use nutrients:

1st week: pour the amount corresponding to the week your plants have and fill the system with the chosen liters (30l in my case);

2nd week: do not change the water in your system completely but add the fertilizers that are indicated for the week corresponding to your cultivation cycle.

Remember to add distilled water to bring the system back to the liters you have chosen (if you mark the water level on the system with a marker, when you have just added the liters you have chosen to use, you can see how much water you need to add to bring back the system to the right capacity).

Always use distilled osmotic water to top up the system.

3rd week: add the fertilizers corresponding to the week you are in without changing the water completely. Top up to bring the system back to the right level.

4th week: completely empty the system by letting out all the water present through the pump or drain hose. Refill the system to the default level and add fertilizers to the week you are in.

Step 5/5 - Constant monitoring of our hydroponic system

Finally, the last step to follow is to constantly monitor our hydroponic systems or systems on a daily basis in order to get the most out of our plants.

Hydroponics, unlike soil cultivation, is much more sensitive to changes in pH and which could change even in a short period, which is why expert growers use pH meters on a monitor to always view the pH of the solution and are able to intervene to change the parameter as soon as possible.

I advise you to keep the pH as close as possible to 5.5 because this is by far the best pH to fully absorb all the nutrients.

So remember to check the pH of your system every day and adjust it with products to bring your value back to the perfect parameter.

If possible, rotate the pots in your system daily or rotate the entire system to get the best light distribution for your plants.

If this is your first experience, we advise you to follow the doses indicated on the fertilizer scheme to avoid excess or nourishment defects, the important thing is to set the pH well to fully absorb the fertilizers and not add them randomly, creating imbalances.

If you want to give your plants a "boost" to get more power, taste and yield, use a boost for flowering (increased potassium) following the doses indicated on the bottle.

CHAPTER 32

CONCLUSIONS

Hydroponics: advantages and disadvantages

The advantages of this technique are greater control over plant development, faster growth and more abundant harvest at any time of the year, maintaining constant production quality and significantly reducing water and fertilizer waste.

Hydroponics accelerates the plant's metabolism, reducing flowering and ripening times since everything the plant needs is always available in the nutrient solution in which the roots are immersed.

In traditional cultivation, most of the water evaporates or is dispersed in the ground until it reaches the aquifers. In agriculture, fertilizers, whether they are bio or "chemical" (everything is chemical ...), can pollute the aforementioned aquifers which in turn can reach lakes or rivers. Fertilizers contain large percentages of nitrogen and phosphorus (essential for plant development). If these substances reached a lake in high concentrations, the entire ecosystem would be altered, allowing algae and bacteria to develop until they consumed all available oxygen, leading to the death of all the fish. This phenomenon is known as eutrophication. Hydroponics, if properly implemented, can eliminate this problem as it requires less fertilizer and the solution is contained, so it does not leach away.

It can be implemented outdoors or indoors The indoor version offers some advantages such as weather resistance, pest control, temperature, humidity and so on. Indoor cultivation is done in greenhouses, sheds, rooms, on the roof of a skyscraper or by converting former semiconductor factories like Fujitsu has done in Japan.

However, an enclosed and therefore dark environment requires artificial lighting using ultraviolet lamps that reproduce solar radiation, entailing a considerable initial and recurring cost (even using photovoltaic modules the problem exists). If it is true that the Sun is free and emits all the necessary frequencies, given that plants have evolved using the Sun, unfortunately it is also true that the Sun is not always available. So we have to transform the light into electricity and then bring it back into uniform and constant light for all our plants in the hydroponic greenhouse. It is very expensive and inefficient... certainly not a trivial problem.

Another advantage for large hydroponic systems is the possibility of installing vertical systems, to increase the yield per square meter by arranging the plants on trays or pipes one above the other.

It is not difficult to imagine a future in which these vertical systems will be installed in every city or even in every district, allowing the production of high quality food on site, reducing costs and pollution due to transport.

Strange beliefs

Many people believe that the plant needs Mother Earth and lots of love to grow. In reality, well-regulated physical parameters are sufficient, such as temperature, visible and ultraviolet electromagnetic radiation and nutrients.

Unfortunately, however, these metaphysical beliefs are so deeply rooted that hydroponic agricultural products are not considered organic, despite the need for herbicides is zero and that of pesticides is greatly reduced, given the absence of the soil which is the main vector of attack for pathogens. Furthermore, if the plants are grown indoors, airborne pathogens will also be greatly reduced, allowing for a more abundant crop without pesticides.

In the future (or maybe even now?) we could even kill the insects that intrude on our hydroponic factory via ultrasound, reducing the use of pesticides to a minimum. Only bacteria and viruses would remain, which can be eliminated by filtering the incoming air and maintaining high standards of hygiene.

Types of hydroponic systems

To date there are many techniques, more or less sophisticated. Here are some of them:

Static or Kratky 's method

Plant roots are only partially immersed in the solution. The solution is not aerated because this method does not include pumps or aerators, so the roots must remain partially uncovered to absorb oxygen. Simple, but there is the risk of generating anoxic environments, good for bacteria, bad for plants that will suffocate. Another risk not to be overlooked are mosquitoes that love stagnant water.

Continuous stream

Plants grow on a perforated tube that continuously carries the nutrient solution. This technique is very scalable, but it is not very resistant to failure, because if the pump fails, the plants risk withering very quickly.

Nutrient Film Technique (NFT)

A variant of the previous one. The difference is in the flow rate of the pump which must be between 1L / min and 2L / min an the slope of the pipe between 1: 1000 and 1:30. These parameters ensure that the solution flows like a thin thread between the roots which remain half in the water and half in the air. This technique perfectly balances the elements required by plants: water, oxygen and nutrients.

Ebb and flow

The roots are periodically flooded with the solution by a pump that is activated with a timer. The frequency of the tides is useful for balancing the relationship between oxygen and nutrients. This technique is also not very resistant to failures, for the same reasons.

Deep Water Culture (DWC)

The roots are completely submerged and oxygen is supplied by a compressor and diffused by porous stones. The aerator is crucial in this technique, because otherwise the plant would wilt very quickly. This technique is more resistant to failure because aerator failure can be stemmed by reducing the solution level, allowing the roots to breathe.

Aeroponics

It works in a similar way to hydroponics, but the plants are suspended in the air, with the dangling roots being periodically sprayed with the nutrient solution by nebulizers. The advantages are many: further reduction of water consumption and the possibility of cultivation without gravity. It is no coincidence that this technique was researched by NASA in the nineties with the Controlled program Ecological Life Support System (CELSS). This technology will most likely be crucial for the next manned space travel.

Fogponics

A variant of aeroponics, in which, by means of ultrasound, a fog is generated, whose droplets have a diameter of less than 10 μm. This way the roots have even more access to oxygen and solution at the same time.

Aquaponics

The union of aquaculture (fish farming) with hydroponics. It is a method that mitigates or eliminates the problems related to the production and disposal of the nutrient solution, through a semi-closed cycle.

The cycle begins with some fish swimming happily in an aquarium eating the feed that is provided to them. After digesting, the fish enrich the water with nitrogen, which is taken and filtered to then reach the plants in hydroponics. The plants absorb the nutrients until the solution runs out and, after another filtering, it is pumped back into the aquarium so that the cycle can continue.

With this system fish and plants are produced, almost completely abolishing the use of fertilizers and, therefore, the risk of damaging the environment. It is a semi-closed cycle, where fish and plants live in a symbiotic relationship. Aquaponics is arguably more delicate, because fish health adds other variables to the equation, but it is extremely efficient.

The nutrient solution

The nutrient solution contains inorganic macroelements and microelements, in well-defined concentrations, as in Hoagland's solution.

To learn more, I highly recommend the Science in Hydroponics website, which contains a lot of valuable information and cutting-edge techniques, always drawing on the latest scientific research in the field.

Macroelements

Macroelements are those absorbed in greater quantities by the plant and are:

nitrogen (N)

phosphorus (P)

potassium (K)

calcium (Ca)

magnesium (Mg)

sulfur (S)

Each plant species likes different concentrations of these elements, but in general the most important parameters are nitrogen, phosphorus and potassium, the so-called NPK concentration expressed in three percentages. Furthermore, during the growth phase the plant needs more nitrogen, while during the flowering phase, more phosphorus.

Microelements

The trace elements are secondary, but necessary for healthy and well-developed plants. Some of these are boron, copper, cobalt, iron, manganese, zinc and molybdenum. Fertilizers for soil typically do not contain many microelements because the plant finds enough in the soil, while in hydroponics they must be added.

Also, more recently, some silicates have been found to be welcome or even necessary for some plants. Soil is rich in silicates, so hydroponic nutrients should also add K_2SiO_3 (potassium silicate), Na_2SiO_3 (sodium silicate) or H_2SiO_3 (orthosilicic acid).

Osmotic pressure

Osmotic pressure is the key factor in a hydroponic nutrient solution, but unfortunately it is very expensive to measure it directly with an osmometer. Therefore, we accept the measurement of electrical conductivity as a guiding parameter, which in practice is very effective. However, it must be remembered that not everything that dissolves in water alters its conductivity, so a solution could be even more hypertonic than the conductivity meter would lead us to believe.

Dissolved oxygen (DO)

A very important parameter for the survival of the plant is the oxygen saturation of the solution. It is good to know that above 35°C the amount of oxygen that can be dissolved in water drops to about 6ppm, which is insufficient in most cases. This assumes that the solution is well ventilated, otherwise the concentration can drop to anoxia and therefore to the suffocation of the plant.

Temperature

As mentioned previously, the temperature of the solution is essential to increase the amount of oxygen that we can supply to the roots of the plant. A temperature between 18°C and 22°C is optimal in terms of quantity of oxygen and resistance of the roots to cold.

Redox potential (ORP)

Redox potential is the measure of a substance's tendency to acquire or lose electrons, and therefore to be oxidized or reduced, and is measured in volts V or millivolts mV.

In hydroponics, this measurement allows you to establish whether the environment is oxidizing enough to keep the various pests at bay, but not too much to cause damage to the plant's roots. For this reason, a value between 300mV and 500mV is optimal for keeping bacteria and fungi away, without destroying the roots. If the ORP value falls below 300mV, it could be an indication of a lack of dissolved oxygen.

One way to increase the ORP is to use hydrogen peroxide or chlorinate the water, remembering, however, that chlorine can kill a plant very quickly, so you have to be very careful with the doses.

Concentration of salts

It must also be said that the plant may not absorb the solution perfectly homogeneously, leading to imbalances and accumulations of salts on the roots of the plant. It is good practice, therefore, to change the nutrient solution regularly.

Alternatively, laboratory analyzes would be required to establish the deficient salts, so that they can be properly reintegrated and the solution recovered. This makes sense, of course, only in large commercial hydroponic plants.

The question arises: why choose hydroponic cultivation if food has always been cultivated in the ground with apparent economic savings?

In reality there are numerous advantages that lead to this choice, but let's look at the most obvious ...

Benefits of hydroponics for everyone

Healthier and stronger daughter plants: plants grown with these systems generate healthier and stronger daughter plants than those grown in the traditional way, so there will be a progressive improvement of the cultivated species.

Natural selection and optimization: each plant species needs environmental and nutritional characteristics that will determine its development.

In hydroponic systems it is possible to recreate them in such a way as to allow the chosen species to develop to the best of its ability.

Control of the nutrient solution: it is possible to control and manage at any time the supply of nutrients that will reach the roots of the plants through the water.

In these hydroculture systems, there is no waste of water, all that is consumed is that actually needed by the plant for its growth, therefore no dispersion in the soil.

Fertilizer saving: the plants will absorb the nutrients received and the rest will remain in the water which will continue to feed the hydroponics, so no dispersions, as for water.

Almost no pesticides: in the optimal conditions reproduced in the hydroponic system, plants will grow in a healthy and rapid way, this will allow a growth free from parasites in most cases, and in any case to deal with any weed in a selective and less aggressive way.

No herbicide: in the pots, there is only space for the plant we grow so there will be no need to weed and consequently not even pollute.

Excellent yield: by being able to feed and grow in an ideal environment, plants will enjoy excellent health and produce more and better, larger specimens, rich in vitamins and flavor.

Root control: being immersed in the nutrient solution and not in the soil, the roots are easily inspected, this allows you to identify any pathogens early and to intervene promptly and more effectively, especially for the cultivation of medicinal plants in which the useful substance is found in the root system.

Biomass: plants grown with hydroponics have a very abundant vegetative phase thanks to the high content of nitrate in the nutrient solution, which is very useful when biomass is needed for various uses, from composting, to the production of fuel.

Extreme conditions: just think that hydroponic modules are used by NASA for space missions to feed astronauts. These systems can integrate everything needed for plant growth, including the rays useful for chlorophyll photosynthesis.

It is obviously not necessary to have extreme situations, but these systems improve and reproduce every nutritional and environmental aspect necessary for the optimal growth of the plant.

We enhance our environment

Little space: thanks to the high efficiency and the right nutritional intake, the plants will not need to compete for survival, therefore the root system will be much less developed than the plants grown on the ground.

This allows for a very high cultivation density per square meter, even in the order of 100 units.

Little physical work: no more heavy bags, hoe, lawn mower and various tools. Physical work is minimal, as well as production waste, this makes hydroponics the perfect system even for those who live in an apartment and have very little space.

Versatile and productive: another aspect to take into consideration is the different need for nutrients of the various species in the various stages of growth, so you can cyclically use a solution used for a type of plant for a phase of its development and then pass it to a other that needs it in a subsequent period simply by changing the container of the nutrient solution.

So - what are you waiting for to start cultivating your vegetable garden?

www.ingramcontent.com/pod-product-compliance
Lightning Source LLC
Chambersburg PA
CBHW071149120626
46546CB00006B/2183